An Antebellum History

Henderson County,

Texas, 1846–1861

by

Kenneth Wayne Howell

EAKIN PRESS ⴸ Fort Worth, Texas
www.EakinPress.com

Copyright © 1999
By Kenneth Wayne Howell
Published By Eakin Press
An Imprint of Wild Horse Media Group
P.O. Box 331779
Fort Worth, Texas 76163
1-817-344-7036
www.EakinPress.com
ALL RIGHTS RESERVED
1 2 3 4 5 6 7 8 9
Paperback ISBN 978-1-57168-337-3
eBook ISBN 978-1-68179-347-4

Library of Congress Cataloging-in-Publication Data

Howell, Kenneth Wayne, 1967-
    Henderson County, Texas : an antebellum history, 1846–1861 / by Kenneth
Wayne Howell.
        p.   c.m.
    Includes bibliographical references and index.
    ISBN 1-57168-337-2
    1. Henderson County (Tex.)—History—19th century. 2. Frontier and pioneer
life—Texas—Henderson County. I. Title.
    F392.H54H69   2000
    976.4'22705--dc21   99-31271
                                                                                              CIP

For

Felesha and Zachary

Contents

Preface

I first attempted to research the early history of Henderson County, Texas, when I was enrolled at Trinity Valley Community College in the late 1980s. My first impulse was to look for general studies of the county in order to obtain basic information. To my great surprise, however, there was only one such work, *History of Henderson County, Texas* by J. J. Faulk. Because I was still an amateur researcher at that time, Faulk's book presented several problems for me. One, the book was difficult to read. It seemed to skip from one topic to another without much cohesion. Second, there was no index in which to look up specific topics. Finally, the study contained little historical analyses of the county's early period. It was at this point that I decided to move toward another topic of study.

A few years later, I took the opportunity, while developing a thesis topic for a master of arts degree at Texas A&M University–Commerce, to explore once again the possibilities of writing a history of the county. By this time, I had learned a great deal more about historical research and was confident that I could write a history of the county. The first step, of course, was to return to Faulk's book, which during my early days at TVCC I had deemed an insignificant study. Upon viewing the book a second time, I quickly began to see its merit. Many minor facts about the county and its people can be found within this study when one looks close enough. In fact, Faulk's study has been cited more times in my work than any other source.

The narrow limits of this book are intentional. The antebellum period has always held my interests and seems to maintain a certain appeal to many readers. Also, there was a need for a more thorough analysis of this period in the county's history. Lack of historical interpretation is one criticism of Faulk's book that I still maintain.

Henderson County illustrates particularly well the story of how frontier settlements in the South were transformed by an influential minority of slaveholders moving west across the southern region of the United States in the antebellum period. The county experienced social, economic, and political changes during the 1850s. These changes were directly related to the county's transformation from a society originally established and governed by yeoman farmers to one controlled by proslavery planting interests. This study examines the county's evolutionary development and explains its reaction to state and national events occurring during the antebellum years.

Unfortunately, there are a limited number of written personal accounts from this time period illustrating day-to-day life in the county. Therefore, instead of focusing on individuals, a greater emphasis has been placed on how social, economic, and political factors affected the population of the county more generally. Since the writing of the original manuscript, however, I have included a sixth chapter which contains several brief biographical sketches of some of the early settlers in the county. I have tried to keep these sketches consistent with the scope of the book, but some of them extend into the Civil War period. Most of the research for chapter six comes from the "Old Settlers Edition" of the *Athens Review* printed on August 2, 1901. Although the biographies are limited and do not include all of the influential people from the county's early history, they will give the reader an insight into the human character of the time period.

I owe a great debt to many people who aided me in the completion of this work. I am most grateful to Dr. James Smallwood of Oklahoma State University who encouraged me to pursue this topic. Dr. Smallwood also shared with me several chapters from his unpublished manuscript on Smith County, Texas. Many thanks go to Dr. Claude Hall of Texas A&M University, College Station, for providing some helpful information on the character of William H. Martin. A special appreciation goes to Dr. Ralph W. Goodwin. This work would not have been possible without his critical reviews and helpful suggestions for its revision. I will not soon forget the patience and guidance Dr. Goodwin gave to this project. I am deeply indebted to Dr. Donald E. Reynolds. During the spring of 1995 at Texas A&M University–Commerce, I was fortunate enough to take Dr. Reynold's graduate class, "Readings in the Old South." His lectures for this class provided me with a foundation in Southern history which has proved invaluable during the course of this study. I am also indebted to Dr. Barry Crouch of Gallaudet University. Dr. Crouch's suggestions greatly improved the historical merit of this work.

Thanks also to Lynn Bell, Bill Rickter, and David A. Baldwin, of the Texas State Archives in Austin for looking up information on certain citizens living in Henderson County during the 1850s. In addition, David Baldwin sent me copies of voter returns from the county during the early 1850s which proved to be very helpful. Deepest thanks to Vesta Hall and Jewel Lambright of the Henderson County Historical Commission. They not only made available the Commission's invaluable collection but also made delightful company during my research visits there. A special thanks goes to Frank La Rue, Jr., Chairman of the Henderson County Historical Commission. Mr. La Rue did much to help insure the historical accuracy of the book. I also want to thank the members of the Henderson County Historical Society for endorsing my book. Though all of the members showed great interest in the work, Arthur Hall, Jo Ann Surls, and John David Broome, members of the Society's editing committee, deserve special credit for their efforts on this project. I am very grateful to all of the librarians and staff members of the Tyler Public Library, the Palestine Public Library, the Henderson County Clint Murchison Memorial Library, the Henderson County Courthouse, the Trinity Valley Community College Library, and especially the James G. Gee Library at Texas A&M University–Commerce. A special appreciation goes to Ben McCartney and John Mills at the Trinity Valley Community College media center. Without their expertise the photographs found in this work would not have been possible. Also, Patrick Davis and Annette Trammell, two very close and dear friends, deserve special recognition for reading my work as it developed.

They offered many valuable insights throughout the writing of this paper.

Finally, I would like to thank my entire family, especially my mother, Jolyn Walters, step-father, Twaine Walters, and sister, Kristie Howell, for their encouragement and support not only during this project but throughout all of my educational experiences. Without them this project would never have been possible. Great appreciation goes to my wife and son. Without their love and support, I would never have finished this book. Felesha, my wife, never complained once about the long hours spent completing this project. Zachary, my son, has given me new found happiness which allowed me to work on this project with renewed energy and enthusiasm.

KENNETH WAYNE HOWELL
Texas A&M University,
June 24, 1999

LIST OF FIGURES

xi

CHAPTER 1

Henderson County, Texas: 1846-1860

The Formative Years

In 1846 TEXAS BEGAN to initiate plans for the reorganization of its interior. During the period of the Republic only a few counties had seemed necessary, but this changed forever with the annexation of Texas into the United States. Local needs now demanded smaller, more effective political units. The state responded by dividing its large territory into smaller counties to improve efficiency and bring more people the opportunity to vote in state and national elections.[1] One of the new counties formed during this time was Henderson County.

On April 27, 1846, the state legislature carved out a large portion of the original Nacogdoches County and named the new area Henderson County after the first governor of Texas, James Pickney Henderson. The new county at first covered an area of approximately 3,500 square miles. Its northern boundary was located along the southern borders of Hunt and Hopkins Counties; the eastern boundary ran along the fringes of Smith and Cherokee Counties and partially along the banks of the Sabine River; the southern boundary was contiguous with Anderson County's northern border; and the western boundary was formed by the Trinity River and Dallas County.[2]

1

"Bush" Wofford home, 1851, Fincastle
— Courtesy of Henderson County Historical Commission

Shortly after the county was created, people began to petition for land grants. On January 26, 1847, Governor Henderson issued a grant for a large plot of land on the east side of the Trinity River to Henry Jefferys, an influential citizen of Cherokee County. Jefferys immediately hired John H. Reagan to survey the land. Reagan, who would later become a prominent political figure in Texas, received 1,750 acres of land and a deed to 114 lots in the proposed town of Buffalo as payment for his services.[3] Jefferys, Reagan, and other prominent citizens began to develop the town of Buffalo with high hopes that the Trinity River would soon be made navigable.[4] These aspirations, however, were never fulfilled, and their dreams of a modern city slowly faded away.

Buffalo disappeared without a trace sometime after the Civil War, leaving no visible evidence of its existence. Its location, however, can be determined by reviewing a variety of sources. These include maps showing places where river boats stopped to trade along the Trinity River, written accounts describing where Acker's Ferry was located on the Trinity, and various references mentioning Buffalo's distance from other towns that are still in existence. These sources point to a general location fifteen miles northwest of the present-day town of Trinidad.[5] Only the memory of the town remains today, but its story is told by a lone state historical marker erected on the spot during the 1980s.

Local officials chose Buffalo as the temporary county seat.[6] The town was a logical choice for officials, because the Trinity made it one of the easiest settlements to access in the county. Since many of the early leaders of the new town were financially secure, they could devote more time and personal concern to county affairs. Finally, the founders of Buffalo, anticipating that river boat traffic would increase, hoped to make the town an economic cornerstone of the county. Clearing the river for traffic would provide farmers a more profitable means for transporting their goods to market. Buffalo, it was thought, would become the major port on the northern end of the Trinity, thus making it a great market city itself. Such a town would have been a perfect location for the county seat. Unfortunately, river improvements were not forthcoming, and the Trinity continued to be too narrow and shallow to support heavy traffic. Thus, the citizens of Buffalo were forced to seek new opportunities elsewhere.[7]

In 1848 state and local officials decided the county government should be moved.[8] This proposal originated when the Texas legislature gave orders to state appointed commissioners

J. M. Pickens home, 1850s, Pickens Spur
— Courtesy of Henderson County Historical Commission

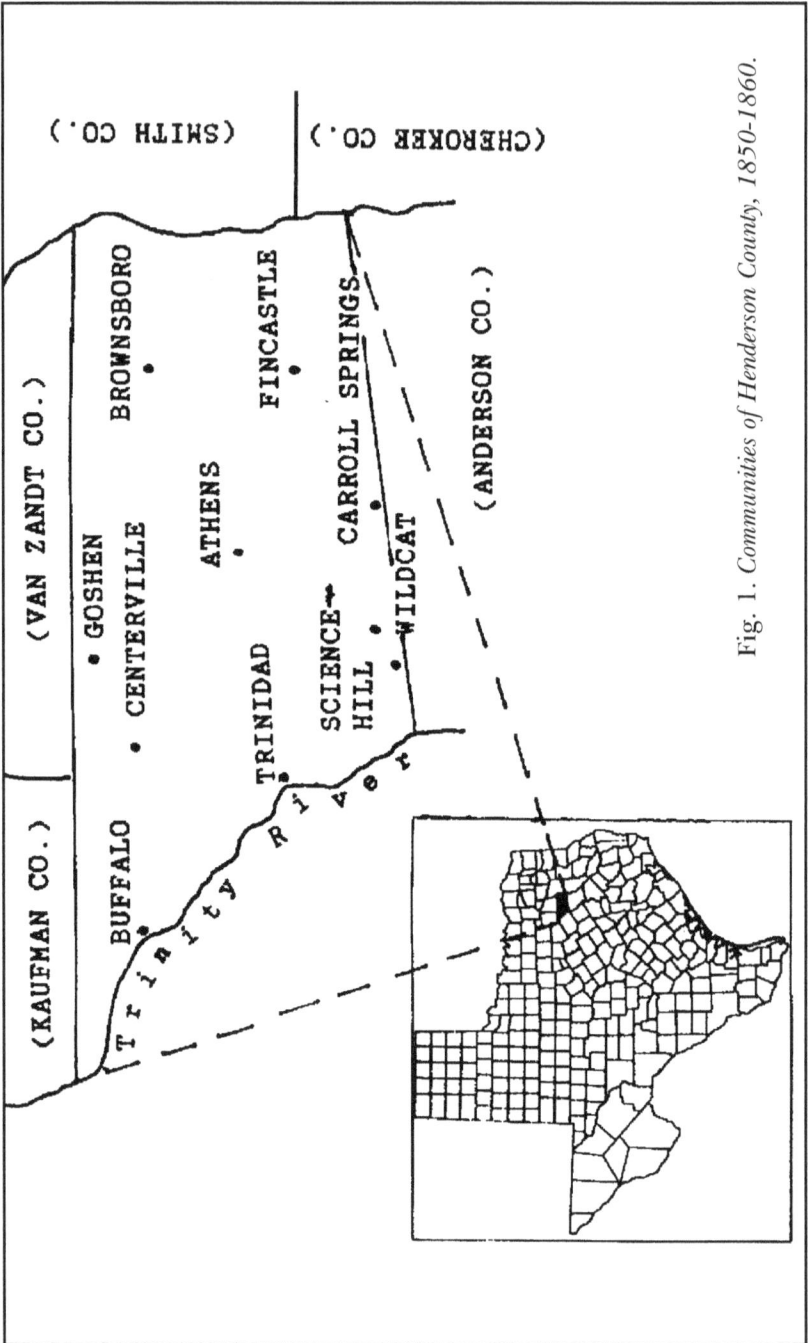

Fig. 1. *Communities of Henderson County, 1850-1860.*

to establish a permanent county seat in the center of the county. Buffalo had been listed as a temporary site. Also Brownsboro, Fincastle, and other growing communities in the eastern part of the county wanted the county seat located closer to them (Fig. 1). Although little in the way of records exists to indicate competition among these communities for control of the local government, it is obvious that a brief power struggle was present.

By examining the county seats of other, more established, East Texas counties, it becomes clear that a great deal was at stake in this struggle between these communities. Towns which became county seats seemed to prosper, grow faster, and achieve stability quicker than the communities around them. This, in part, explains why the local government in Henderson County moved to three different locations between 1846 and 1850.

In March 1848, under the direction of the state legislature, county officials gave David E. Mallard, Dr. S. Graham, John Baker, and Dr. H. M. Allen the task of determining the center of the county. Once they had established a central point, the committee was to nominate a place within five miles of it as a permanent location for the county seat. They found the central point with little trouble and, in accordance with their instructions, suggested a possible site for the government, later known as Centerville. Having fulfilled its prescribed assignment, the committee itself recommended that Buffalo remain the county seat. No doubt this was in response to strong pressure from prominent citizens of that community. But voters participating in a county-wide election favored the more central location, Centerville. When the commissioners' court gave the order to move all of the legal documents to the new site, the citizens of Buffalo protested. Buffalo's spokesmen, led by Andrew F. McCarty, argued before the commissioners' court that election officials had excluded the voters in and immediately around their community.[9] The court patiently listened to these arguments, then continued with their plans to move.

Centerville was located twelve miles northeast of Buffalo. One reason for moving to this new location was John Starr's generous donation of one hundred acres of land. The county seat was to be built on this land with visions of a great town to

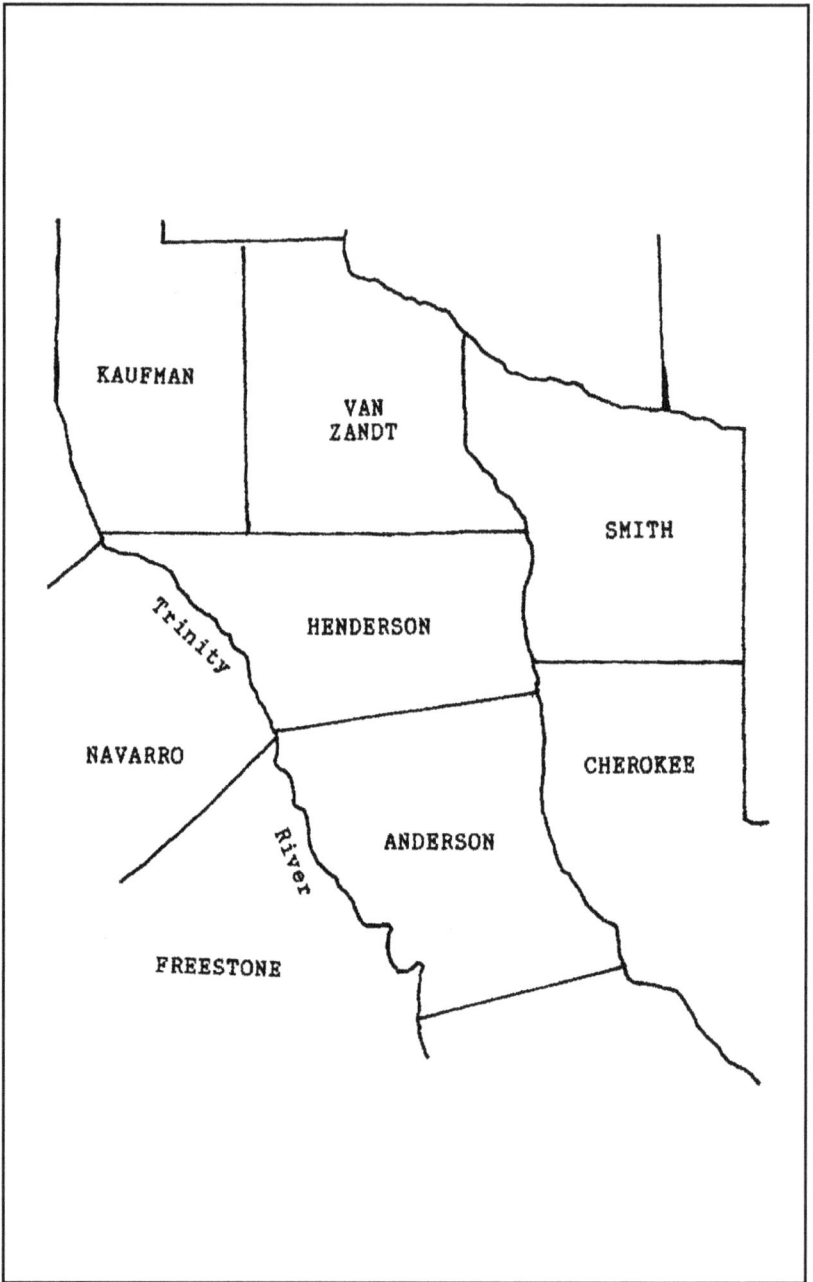

Fig. 2. *Established counties which surrounded Henderson County in 1860.*

follow. The location was quickly surveyed into blocks and lots, and the county clerk's office was assigned to a cabin which cost the taxpayers fifty dollars to build. County commissioners held the first term of court in their new home in September 1848.

Unfortunately for Centerville, its time was limited both as the county seat and a town. The people of Buffalo successfully influenced the court to move back to its former site in May 1850—probably due to McCarty's original protest being reviewed by a higher court of law. Also, the fledgling town offered few comforts. Such crude conditions in Centerville, no doubt, were another factor contributing to the court's decision to move back to Buffalo.[10]

In October, of the same year, the court moved yet again. This move became necessary in response to a new act passed through the state legislature reducing the county to its present size (Fig. 2). Several new counties, Kaufman, Van Zandt, Rockwall, and Rains, were now cut away to its north. The county lost approximately 2,560 square miles as a result, and a newly formed town called Athens now became the central point of the county.[11] In all likelihood pressure once again from the eastern portion of the county as well as from the state legislature forced the court to look for a central location. Shortly afterward, the town of Athens was chosen as the permanent home of the county seat.[12]

Most communities within Henderson County shared many similarities. Buildings, roads, and modern conveniences were few in the early days of these settlements. Farming was the leading industry, along with a few developing mercantile businesses. Some localities had schools, but these were primitive in nature. Such communities struggled to survive the frontier environment. Some enjoyed remarkable success while others, such as Buffalo, disappeared completely.

At the time it became the county seat, Athens was no different than any of the other towns in the county. News of the court's decision came at a time when the town was still in its early stages of development. Only a few months earlier Samuel Huffer had completed his survey of the area. The town's central location, however, allowed county officials to serve the needs of the entire county including the eastern parts of the county that

Rev. & Mrs. W. B. Stirman, arrived in Henderson County in 1848.
— Courtesy of Henderson County Historical Commission

had been previously neglected. At this time the county's approximate population stood at 1,160 free inhabitants and 81 slaves.[13]

The court wasted little time in getting down to business. Before a courthouse could be built, Judge O. M. Roberts handed down legal decisions under the shade of a large oak tree. In October of 1850, the commissioners' court quickly addressed this problem by contracting with John Loop to build a municipal building for the sum of sixty-five dollars. He completed the task on November 19, 1850.[14] Athens quickly evolved into one of the more successful communities within the county. There seem to have been two reasons for this success. Its location was convenient to all areas of the county, and, of course, it was now the home of the county's judicial system.[15]

Athens and Buffalo were not the only noted towns in Henderson County. Southwest of Athens was a place known as Science Hill. Reverend Hezekiah Mitcham, a Methodist minister, had established this community in 1848. Within the same year the citizens built a Masonic Lodge and a school, Science Hill Academy. This school was designed to serve the educational needs of the children at Science Hill and the small nearby village of Wildcat.[16]

Brownsboro, another aspiring community in the county, was located approximately fifteen miles northeast of Athens on Kickapoo Creek. A promoter named John "Red" Brown was among the first to settle this site in 1849. By 1860 the area supported a stable but small population. Many of the community's citizens were immigrants from Scandinavia. Most of the people of Brownsboro were farmers, but there were also a few small shopkeepers. James Brian and Jack Bridges opened the first businesses within the community, a saloon and a general store respectively. Also, W. L. McNeill, reportedly one of the most prosperous men in the county, owned a dry goods store in Brownsboro. The town even had its own physician, Dr. D. M. Wier.[17]

Fincastle, another growing community in the county, was located nineteen miles southeast of Athens on the J. J. Martinez survey. Between 1852 and 1867 this town had one of the strongest economies in the county, supporting a general mercantile store, a liquor and grocery store, a blacksmith shop, a cotton gin, and a grist mill. The community's supplies came from the towns of Marshall and Jefferson, and its mail came from Athens by horse and rider.[18]

Two more small settlements located in the county were Goshen and Trinidad. Just like other small communities within the county during this time, these were sparsely populated farming communities in the early stages of development. Goshen was located in the northwest part of the county near the Van Zandt County line.[19] Trinidad was located approximately fifteen miles west of Athens on the Trinity River. Because the area was easier to farm, Goshen, at least in the early history of the county, became more prosperous and populated of the two settlements. Outside of a few farmers, the area around Trinidad was sparsely populated. The most logical reason for the relatively small number of inhabitants living and farming in this area was the sporadic flooding of the lowlands which surrounded the fledgling river town. There was only one building in Trinidad of commercial significance—a cotton shed near the river. Farmers would store their bales of cotton in this shed until there was enough rainfall to make it possible to float them down the river on large rafts. In the long run, however, such an irregular method of shipping cotton to market proved unprofitable and was eventually abandoned.[20]

The roads of Henderson County were like most during this same period in Texas—terrible. Travelers often cursed the condition and scarcity of roads in Texas. It was next to impossible to traverse the countryside in lightweight buggies and carriages because of the mud, tree stumps, and washed out trails. Henderson County's first roads were no doubt just as primitive. According to J. J. Faulk's *History of Henderson County*, the original roads merely followed old "trails made by the Indians, buffalos, and wild horses."[21] Improvements to the existing roads came slowly, and new roads were laid out only as they were needed. One reason why road construction took so long was that the landowners themselves were responsible for road maintenance. Their families and slaves worked on the roads during slack times in the growing season.[22]

Considering the descriptions of the roads, it is obvious that the owners devoted little time to maintaining them. Yet the newer roads were a considerable improvement over the old trails used by the earliest settlers. The new routes were laid out to connect emerging towns and tended to be straighter than the older trails.[23] In 1850 the most recently completed road in the county ran from Buffalo to Larrissa, a small town in the northern part of Cherokee County.[24]

Society and Culture

The population of Henderson County during this period was a diverse group of individuals from several states and foreign countries. The 1850 Census indicates there were 1,157 free people and 81 slaves living within the county. Eighty-five percent of the adults had been born in the South—38 percent in the Lower South and 47 percent in the Upper South.[25] Two studies that discuss migration patterns into East Texas are Walter Buenger's "Secession Revisited: The Texas Experience" and Richard G. Lowe and Randolph B. Campbell's *Planters & Plain Folk: Agriculture in Antebellum Texas*. Buenger's study maintains that most people in East Texas migrated from the Lower South.[26] Lowe and Campbell, on the other hand, indicate that more East Texans arrived from the Upper South.[27] The facts, in regard to Henderson County, seem to support Buenger's study. Many settlers moved from their birthplaces to live in other states before finally migrating to Texas. One must determine the last state of residence for migrants in order to understand the migratory patterns of the people moving into the county. This can be accomplished by looking at the birthplaces of the inhabitants' children. According to the children's birthplaces in the 1850 census, approximately 50 percent of the families that moved to Henderson County came from the Lower South, especially from Arkansas and Alabama. Those from the Upper South made up only about 35 percent of the county's population. The remaining 15

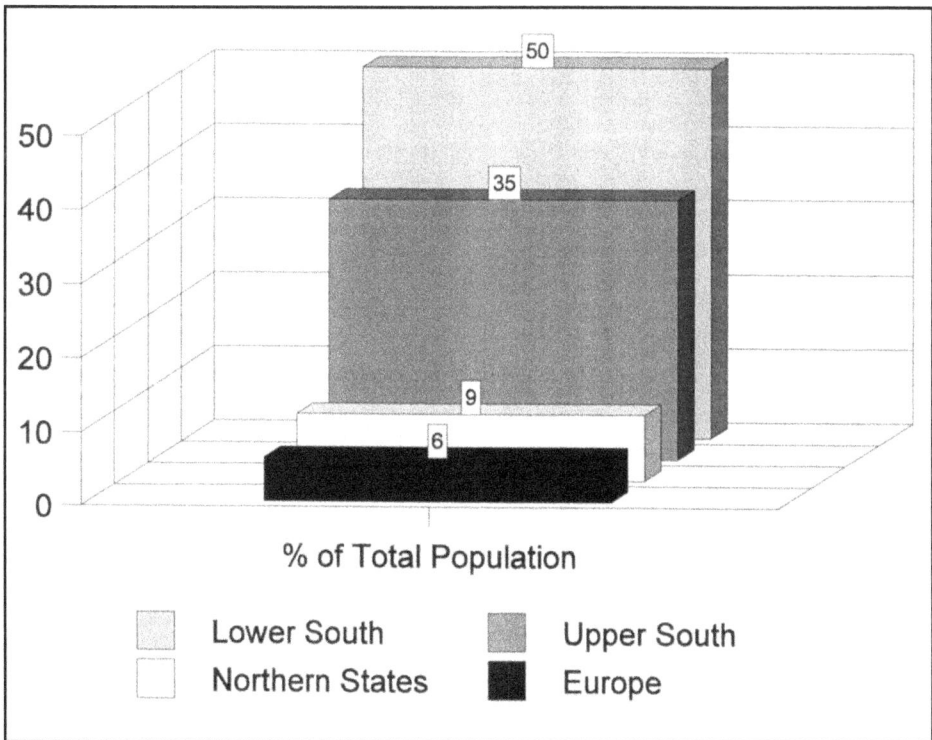

Fig. 3. *Migration into Henderson County, Texas, 1850. This graph is based on the birthplaces of the inhabitants' children, according to the 1850 census records for Henderson County, Texas.*

Ole and Kristi (Tjostelsdatter) Olson
— Courtesy of Henderson County Historical Commission

percent of the population came from either northern states in the United States or from Europe. Northerners made up about 9 percent of the population, and foreigners constituted another 6 percent (Fig. 3).[28]

Regardless of their origins, many people corresponded with the relatives they left behind and were able to persuade them, especially those living in the South, to come to Texas. Their methods of persuasion varied. Some talked of the rich soil; others mentioned the cheap land prices; and still others alluded to the possibilities for gaining prominence and wealth.

Henderson County's early settlers developed an unique way of life. Most received mail less than two or three times a year, and the nearest newspaper was in the next county. Thus what news they received from the outside world came largely by word of mouth. These isolated conditions, however, may actually have worked in their favor by forcing neighbors to depend heavily upon one another. Such cooperation often helped them pull through hard times.

Religion

The people of Henderson County understood the value of religion. Early Christian settlers enjoyed and needed both spiritual guidance and fellowship. John A. Edwards suggests that "many Texans viewed the church as a social agent offering cultural events" along with "educational experiences" and "leisure activities."[29] This was especially true in newly formed areas like Henderson County. It is interesting to note that the people remained faithful Christians even when the church preached against the few entertainments available to them—drinking, gambling, horse-racing, and dancing.[30]

During the 1850s the three primary religious denominations in Henderson County were the Baptists, the Cumberland Presbyterians, and the Methodists. The Baptist Church clearly had the strongest following in the early history of the county. In 1858 the first sanctuary in the county, "The Bethel Church," was built in Athens by the Baptists. Accordingly, their building was erected "on the street leading to the local cemetery."[31]

Although the Baptists owned the first church building in Athens, other religious denominations were permitted to use it and also undoubtedly contributed to its upkeep. To avoid doctrinal differences, preachers of the various sects were allowed equal time in the pulpit. One church member recalled:

> In those early days, it seems, that church relations made but little difference, as the Methodists and Presbyterians worshiped there just as freely as the Baptists, which continued for many years afterward. I have heard Uncle Dick Watkins preach there many times. His habit was to exhaust his subjects in every sermon. We could always tell when he reached the high-water mark [of his sermon]. He would say "now in conclusion." . . . We had no organs or instrumental music to assist in the singing, this was in the days of the lining of the hymns by the preacher, who was generally the leader; and the choir was composed of the whole congregation; and it seems to me now, that everybody sang with zest and vigor. We had a Sunday school composed of members of the different churches, all was agreeable and all went merry as a marriage bell.[32]

Churches did their best to fulfill the religious needs of the people in Henderson County—including slaves. Documentation indicating that churches accepted slaves as members is sparse, but some church records refer to "colored members."[33] Randolph Campbell's *An Empire for Slavery: The Peculiar Institution in Texas, 1821-1865* points out that it was common for East Texas slaves to belong to organized churches.[34] After all, saving souls was the Christian's responsibility, regardless of whether the soul belonged to a slave or a freeman. Though many Baptists were willing to preach to the bondsmen, few were disposed to give them freedom. In fact, most southern Baptists remained staunch defenders of the institution of slavery.

In May of 1855, a minister of the Cumberland Presbyterian Church, Reverend Robert Hodge, began to preach to the citizens of Athens. The good reverend and his family had moved to Henderson County in the early 1850s with the intent of starting a Presbyterian church. Reverend Hodge no doubt considered Athens a promising site for his church because of its location in the center of the county. It should be noted that Presbyterian efforts within the county actually pre-dated that of the Baptists. They did not, however, build a sanctuary of their own until well after the 1860s.

Between 1855 and 1868 the membership of the Presbyterian church grew from nine people to eighty-five. In order to keep up with the increasing size of the congregation, the church had to make several moves. First, they moved from their original location, a small frame building on the south side of the square that also served as the county court house, to the Masonic Lodge. They remained there until after the construction of the Baptist sanctuary. At that time, the Presbyterians joined the Baptists in Sunday worship until they could build their own meeting house.

On December 13, 1857, the Presbyterians organized a committee to oversee construction of a church building of their own. Members on this committee included Nat P. Coleman, Dr. William Kerr, P. S. Bethel, and William M. Gray. It is not clear what happened, but the Presbyterians did not actually build a sanctuary until 1881.[35] More than likely, the Civil War and Reconstruction delayed their efforts.

Before 1860 the Methodists began to become a powerful

force throughout the South, especially with the slaveholding class.[36] In 1859 Methodists organized the Methodist Church in Henderson County as a branch of the Palestine district, but they did not build a church building of their own in Athens until 1884. Also in 1859 twelve congregations worshiped on a regular basis in Henderson County. Often, the services were held at a member's house or in one of the local school houses. The following is a list of Methodist church congregations within the county:

Athens Church	47 members
Mitcham Campground	18 members
Walnut Creek Church	18 members
(6 colored members)	
Gilmore Chapel	17 members
Price's Chapel	18 members
County Line Church	15 members
Tindel's School House	16 members
Flat Creek Church	8 members
McCostlin Church	17 members
Powers School House	7 members

* Two Methodist churches were located in Fincastle.[37]

Education

Science Hill Academy, established in 1848 for the people living in the community of Wildcat, was one of the first schools in Henderson County. In all likelihood the academy was a church-sponsored school since the Reverend Hezekiah Mitcham, a Methodist minister, was responsible for establishing the school. J. J. Faulk claimed that the academy "was at one time the leading educational center for the county."[38]

During the 1850s the Masons built the first schoolhouse of importance in Athens. This was a two-story structure located on Palestine Street. The facility was designed to serve two purposes. The lower floor was made into classrooms for the school, and the upper floor was used for Masonic meetings.[39]

The people of Fincastle constructed their first school in 1852. It was like most rural schools of the day.

> . . . a common log house about eighteen feet square, sills and plates were solid hewn logs, gables weather boarded with long boards; cracks in the walls were covered with boards and roof covered with red oak boards; ordinary benches or seats were made of planks, writing desk consisted of a long plank fastened to one end of the house, so that the children could reach it by either standing or sitting on one of the rude benches.[40]

For the most part, Henderson County students had similar educational experiences regardless of where they attended school. Pupils were expected to supply their own ink, pens, and paper. Their first task was to learn how to read. The process began with students learning the alphabet. The next objective was to combine vowels and to form the phonic sound patterns of English. Following the pronunciation lesson, the students began to learn individual words, beginning with simple two syllable words and later advancing to words of three and four syllables. Later, students began to put primary sentences together. Before long the class was reading passages from textbooks, including the famous *McGuffy Readers*.[41]

As they learned to read, the students also began to practice writing. This task was difficult for the young learners. Normally, a student learning to write spent many hours repeatedly copying letters, words, and sentences from different grammar textbooks.[42] Understandably, these lessons were unpopular with the children. J. J. Faulk recalled the following about his early writing lessons:

> Now you may talk about solving difficult problems, but this [learning to write] is the hardest one I ever encountered; while it was almost murder to the little fellows—it is really funny to look back on it and see them trying to copy. . . . They tried but they could not hold the pen staff right in their little fingers, and it was just impossible for them to look at their writing and look at the copy at the same time. Some would keep their seats, some would stand up and some lean over on the desk and many of them would lick their tongues out and raise their bodies up off the seat every time they made a letter. . . . This

half hour's torture nearly gave us the cramps and when the half hour was up each sprang up like rubber balls.[43]

Only the most basic mathematic skills were part of these early school programs. Students were expected to learn simple addition, subtraction, multiplication, and division. These lessons were considered vital to the future business success of each student. The teachers developed their lessons from the popular text *Smiley's Arithmetic*.[44]

During the 1850s there was a growing interest throughout Texas for improvements in education. The state legislature under the leadership of Governor Elisha M. Pease responded by passing several acts to provide funding for public schools.[45] Unfortunately, the war disrupted these efforts before they could take full effect. However, these beginnings helped shape future plans for the schools after the Civil War.

Entertainment

During the early period of settlement, most people were forced to devote many long hours to the drudgery of back-breaking physical labor. Only a small portion of time could be devoted to relaxation. Children normally had more time than anyone to participate in social activities.

Growing up, children enjoyed a variety of games. Some of the games they played included town ball (baseball), bull pen (dodge ball), and jumping (long-jump.) Of these three, town ball was the more popular. The children used a paddle three feet in length for batting the ball. Trees growing in a circular pattern served as the bases. J. J. Faulk described one such playing field, "First [base] was a big black jack, second one was a hickory, third one was a black jack (most easterly one), fourth was a hickory and next one was home."[46]

Another favorite pastime, especially for the boys, was swimming in washed out places along the banks of rivers and creeks. They would strip off their clothing and jump into a calm pool of water. Faulk recalled swimming in "the old wash hole . . . on

Tindel's creek, it was called the Old Eddy. We ran all the way there and by the time we got there we were nude and our clothes were dropped on the bank and in we went."[47]

Both boys and girls played the game known as "follow," an exaggerated version of the more traditional game of follow-the-leader. The object was for the leader to make it impossible for the others to follow. A leader might lead his group across creeks, up and down trees, and through a variety of other unpleasant places to make them give up the chase.[48]

Perhaps the most interesting game played by the children of Henderson County was "shinny" which was a form of land hockey. The game required an incredible amount of coordination and endurance from its participants. Because of the physical demands of this game those who participated often went home with a collection of bruises. Most of the injuries resulted when one player struck another with his playing stick.[49]

Adults in Henderson County enjoyed many entertainments common throughout East Texas. They read newspapers which contained poems and stories. People grew fond of books by well-established authors and enjoyed receiving letters from relatives and friends.[50] Almost every family had at least one member who could read living with them, so that even those who were illiterate could still enjoy someone reading to them. More than likely, available books were shared with neighbors, and letters from relatives came several times a year.

Reading materials were a prized possession to the early settlers. During the 1850s the only newspaper readily available in Henderson County was the *Trinity Advocate* edited and published in Palestine by James Ewing. Ewing often traveled throughout the county delivering his weekly paper, always on the lookout for new subscribers.[51]

Many people of course found leisure in visiting with family and friends. They often gathered together at social functions. One Athenian recalled, "During those times the people would meet nearly every Sunday evening at the court house and sing fa, so, la songs. It was great singing, everybody joined. First one and then another would lead, using a forked iron instrument to get the sound."[52]

Often such crowds gathered to watch the performances of

the illustrious Dr. D. C. Bellows, a professed phrenologist, who entertained the community with his claim to reveal people's personalities and habits by feeling the shapes and bumps of their heads.[53]

Texas families also celebrated many of the national holidays, especially after annexation. Some of the more popular holidays were July the Fourth, Christmas, New Year's Day, Thanksgiving, and May Day. No records show that the slaves of Henderson County joined in the celebration of these holidays, but it was not uncommon in East Texas for them to do so.[54]

Societies

The only formal social organization of any note in Henderson County during the formative period was the Masonic Order. The first Masonic Lodge was organized at Science Hill in 1848. The next was in Athens in the early 1850s. According to one early Mason of Henderson County "in the beginning, only the best men were allowed to become members and [they] had to have a mighty white record even at that."[55] Masons were actively involved in both educational and religious affairs of the community. In part, the Masons worked to improve the community from a sense of duty to themselves. They made vows to maintain a certain quality of life for all Masonic members to enjoy. Thus they committed themselves to promote good works in their local communities and accepted a responsibility to help all citizens reach their full potential.

A short-lived social/intellectual society also worth mentioning was the Buffalo Lyceum. Between 1846 and 1850, a small number of men living in the northwestern portion of the county began to hold regular meetings to exercise their powers of thought and argument. The minutes of the society's meetings suggest that the members were learned men.[56] They debated such topics as: "Is it a good policy in the government of Texas to grant colony contracts?"; "Whether it is a better policy to clean out the Trinity River now, or wait until we raise a surplus quantity of produce to ship off?"; "Is love a stronger passion than anger?"; and "Should capital punishment be abolished?"[57]

CHAPTER 2

Economics of the County: 1846-1860

Wealth of the County

EVEN THOUGH COTTON production and land speculation were already central to the Texas economy, the historian Walter L. Buenger in his study of the Texas secession crisis maintains that Texas during the 1850s was less mature economically, socially, and politically than any of the other Lower South states.[1] This certainly seems to have been true for Henderson County. The county strongly resembled other southern counties during their formative years. As in the earlier frontier days of these older southern counties, there were as yet no truly large planters in Henderson County. According to the 1850 census the largest property holder in the county held $5,000 worth of real estate. His tract of land was just over 2,000 acres in size. During this period in East Texas this was equivalent to the land holdings of a middle-size planter.[2] Also just as in the earlier periods of older frontier areas in the South, the obligations of most taxpayers were relatively light because they had small farms. The 1860 census estimated the taxable values of the county at $2,114,874. This valuation broke down into approximately $1,464,179 in personal property and another $650,695 in livestock. Most southern frontier regions were sparsely settled. Henderson County ranked fiftieth in population among the eighty counties of Texas.[3] The county began very much like so many others in the Old South, a struggling farming society existing on subsistence farming while trying to capitalize on cash crops.

Farmers and Farming

Most of Henderson County's wealth came from agriculture. Either directly or indirectly, the county's population depended on farming. During the antebellum period, men were judged on how well they managed their farms and marketed their crops. Those who enlarged their farms and produced more than the previous year were held in high regard. Those who did not were considered failures. R. D. Palmer, a resident from a small farming community in the southern part of the county, recalled:

> Ten or fifteen acres was taken in [the] first year and year after year the farm grew larger, so that in a few years we had a good size farm. It was said then that if a man let his farm grow smaller he was no good, but if a farmer wanted to keep in good repute he should make his farm a little larger every year.[4]

Henderson County farmers fit primarily into two classifications, yeoman farmers and small planters. According to figures in the 1850 Census, most of the early settlers were yeoman farmers.[5] A yeoman farmer and his family usually worked their farm without the aid of slave labor. For such people wealth meant owning a plot of land and the necessary equipment needed to work it. An industrious man, it was thought, needed only to use his land and equipment to provide an adequate living for his family.

Middle-size farmers or small planters were those who held lands valued between $500 and $9,999.[6] In 1850 fifty-two settlers in Henderson County fit this classification. Some twenty-six held $1,000 or more in real estate property.[7] Because of the absence of large plantations, it can be assumed that cash crops were not being exported from Henderson County in large quantities during the early 1850s. It does not follow, however, that commercial crops were not grown at all during this period. The production of cotton did begin to increase toward the late 1850s. The county's cotton production grew from 31 bales in 1850 to 2,105 bales in 1860.[8] The men responsible for this rise in production were the middle-size farmers. Their search for markets was one reason why the people of Buffalo thought the Trinity River might be made navigable. Since only a limited number of people could afford to farm commercially, most must be considered subsistence farmers. For people living in near-frontier conditions, their first concern was survival.

The farming techniques used by the people of Henderson County determined the economic success of their community. The initial task of the farmer was to prepare his fields for cultivation. The land had to be cleared of unwanted obstructions, such as trees, brush, and rocks. This often proved to be difficult work.[9]

Plowing the fields came next. Usually plowing began sometime in January. First, the farmers plowed long rows approximately six feet apart; thereafter, they used lighter plows to make shallow furrows on top of the rows. This was known as setting the seed bed. This process usually continued until February or March. After placing the seeds in the furrows, the farmer covered them with a harrow. One Henderson County man recalled his early days working with his father on their family farm:

> [The] ground had to be cleared and fenced for farms, and this was very hard work. The bushes undergrowth and small trees had to be cut down and burned. All farms were fenced by rails, generally eight feet long. They were split from large trees, cut up into right lengths, using iron wedges, gluts, and heavy mauls to split the rails, and they had to be put up so as to keep out hogs and cattle. . . . We rented land the first year . . . Georgia plow stocks and straight shovels and bull tongues were the farming implements. Oxen were used for plowing and it was mighty hard, slow work.[10]

Cultivation began when the crops started breaking through the ground. Using a lightweight plow, the farmer broke the ground between the rows in order to remove the grass and weeds. A hoe was used for the same purpose up closer to the plants. This process went on through June. If corn was the crop planted, it would be harvested around June or July. If the crop was cotton, then harvesting began early in August and continued through December.[11] Providing that these crops were not damaged from the weeds, worms, drought, or floods, a farmer might produce enough to earn a profit.

The main staple crop grown in Henderson County was corn. The eastern part of the county, known as the "Egypt of Henderson County," produced the largest volume of corn and wheat within the county.[12] But corn was only one of many other foods grown within the county. The county, like many of its neighboring counties, also produced sweet potatoes, Irish potatoes, peas, beans, okra, and squash. Some East Texas historians believe that sweet potatoes were second only to corn in production.[13]

Livestock were another important source of subsistence to the people of Henderson County. For the most part the livestock ran wild in the woods that surrounded the farms. Although the animals during this period held little market value, they were a valuable source of food. The primary animals eaten by the settlers were cattle, hogs, and peccaries. Most frontier settlers mistakenly called the peccary, or javelina, a wild hog. Though related to the pig, the peccary is not part of the swine family. Nevertheless, both peccaries and wild hogs, mostly razorbacks, ran wild in the woods and were hunted during the fall.[14] Palmer recalled that "hogs and cattle were plentiful, raised in the woods on the range. When a beef was killed, it was dried by the fire to keep it."[15] The settlers used animal skins for a variety of things. How these skins were processed will be discussed later in this chapter.

The Cotton Industry and Other Prominent Businesses Within the County

The cotton industry in Henderson County did not fully mature until sometime after the Civil War. However, evidence proves that cotton was produced on a small scale much earlier. Despite low levels of production in the 1850s, the cultivation of cotton gradually increased within the county. Money earned from the county's exports helped strengthen the local economy. The amount of money attributed to cotton production grew from $4,200 in 1850 to $410,475 in 1860.[16] Partially this occurred because of an increase of 2,074 acres planted in cotton. Interestingly, this increase in the county's cash flow may not have stayed within the county. Because farmers sold their cotton to markets outside of the county, a substantial portion of their profit went to pay the fees of agents located in large cities like Houston, Galveston, and Shreveport.

It was a common practice for small farmers to market their crops through such "factors" or commission merchants in larger towns.[17] These agents helped the farmers in a variety of ways. First, they took the farmer's cotton and stored it in a warehouse until it could be sold for a good price. After selling the cotton they promptly sent the income to the planter minus their fees. Second, the "factors" sometimes purchased goods for the planters. Often these purchases were deducted from the farmer's income. Third, the agents often made secured loans to the planters. The agents usually accepted the next cotton crop as collateral. Finally, the agents often took care of the farmer's business in town, mailing letters, placing advertisements in newspapers, and arranging meetings with lawyers.[18] Another option that was popular, especially with the small planters, was to sell their crops to a local merchant in a nearby town. The merchants in turn processed the cotton on their own accounts.[19]

One business directly related to cotton growing was cotton ginning. Once the cotton was harvested, it was taken to a gin where the seeds were extracted from the lint. Afterward, the cotton was pressed into bales each weighing 400 to 600 pounds.[20] Generally speaking, the early cotton gins were housed in three-story buildings. Cotton seed which had been removed from the lint was stored on the top floor. The middle floor contained the gin. Located on the ground floor was a large wooden wheel which served as the source of power for the gin.[21] This wheel was usually turned by mules. There were few gins in Henderson County during the 1850s. The only two mentioned in local histories were located in the eastern part of the county at Fincastle and New York.

Some of the smaller cotton producers in the county probably did not carry their cotton to a gin, since their small amounts of cotton would not cover the expense of the trip. Instead many of these small farmers sold their cotton directly to nearby owners of larger farms, who either owned their own gins or produced enough cotton to justify having it processed at one of the local gins. This was probably the case along the southern county line near the larger farms located in Anderson County.[22]

Cotton, though grown in Henderson County, was not a major factor in its economy during the 1850s. There were several reasons for this. First, late in the 1850s East Texas suffered a long drought. Second, many of the county's best soils were overlooked because of the common belief that only the wooded areas were fertile enough for cotton production. Finally, the county's location made it hard to transport crops to market. Although the county had two major river systems, neither was navigable the entire year. As suggested in the previous chapter, heavy rains were required to make the Trinity navigable.[23]

The only other method for transporting crops was overland. It is evident, by the number of wagoners listed in the 1860 census, that this method was fairly popular in Henderson County. Such men carried the county's harvest on the long journey to Shreveport, Louisiana, the closest market. This annual trip began as soon as the cotton was baled and loaded on the wagon. Oxen, having more endurance than horses, were used to pull the wagons on this tortuous journey. In Shreveport, Texas farmers usually received eight to ten cents a pound for their cotton.[24]

Cotton production, though limited in the county, did make some small contributions to the economy of Henderson County. It increased the wealth of the county and allowed at least a few individuals to acquire moderate land holdings. But perhaps its greatest contribution was that it tied the county to the Old South both economically and politically. Hope for future profits in cotton production was a primary reason why the Confederate cause received so much support from the county as the Civil War began.[25]

There were many other economic opportunities available to the people of Henderson County. Blacksmith shops, brick and pottery companies, tanning yards, mills, general merchant stores, and hotels were located within the county during the 1850s. Usually these ventures were small and operated by single families.[26]

Blacksmith shops and mills were mainly located near the farming centers of the county. The primary job of the blacksmith was to make, mend, and repair the different tools the farmer used in growing his crops. A good blacksmith was important for the economic success of each community.[27]

Milling was another important industry in the county. Farmers depended on the mills to process the corn and grains they produced. Many of the county's mills, like its cotton gins, were powered by mules or horses. However, some mills took advantage of the swift moving creeks located on the watershed of the Trinity River for their power source. J. B. Hogg's mill, seven miles southeast of Athens on Mine Creek, was one of several mills located within the county. It was reported that Hogg's mill ground all of the corn of the farmers in that area.[28]

Another type of mill located within the county was the saw mill. One such mill was housed in Brownsboro. It was owned by the Reiersons, a prominent Norwegian family of that area. Their mill supplied most of the lumber used within the county.[29]

Tanning leather was another common business throughout the East Texas area. The tan yards were responsible for processing raw animal hides. This process involved soaking the hides in tubs of specially prepared water. This water-based solution, made by soaking the bark of oak or sumac trees, tanned and softened the leather. In order to preserve the leather,

Jens Lasson Reierson
— Courtesy of Henderson County
Historical Commission

the tanners salted the raw side of the skin as soon as it was removed from the animal.

Tanned leather was used for a variety of products in the 1850s, most commonly clothes, upholstery, and rugs. The most frequently used hides were those of the bear, buffalo, and cattle.[30] One man remembered that his father and brothers "used to hire [themselves out] to old man Carroll who ran a tan yard at Carroll Springs;" his brother "Jim learned to make saddle trees and he was detailed during the Confederate war to make saddles for the soldiers."[31]

A small number of other businesses appeared in the towns of the county before the 1860s. These included the general merchant stores and hotels. A. W. Meredith, who had lived in Athens during the 1850s, described the town's general stores in a letter to local historian J. J. Faulk: ". . . dry goods, plows, and farming implements on the same shelves near each other. It was thought that a merchant should carry everything for sale from a cambric needle to a cannon, and they generally had in the back room a barrel with a tin cup to quench the thirst of their customers."[32]

The first hotel in the county was built in Athens by Joab McManus. It was a simple boarding house and tavern located on the northeast corner of the square.[33] The hotel was probably one of a kind in the county during this period. Such a hotel was not the only place where one could find room and board. Many people opened up their homes to travelers, offering food and shelter in return for work or money.

Other industries within the county were more specialized. Among these were brick kilns and pottery workshops. The first potter in the county was Levi Cogburn. He located his shop on the outskirts of Athens near a little spring. Cogburn opened his business in 1857 and continued it until he died in 1866.[34] W. C. Bobo opened the first brick kiln in Athens about this same time. From this kiln came much of the brick used to build some of the early structures around Athens.[35]

During the 1850s Henderson County's economy was establishing itself rapidly. Mills, small craft shops, and country stores sprang up in most communities, and the cotton industry was beginning to gain momentum. With the coming of the Civil War, however, this emerging commercial economy would almost disappear. The main reason for the economic shutdown was the loss of manpower. The war required the fittest men for military service and left the rest, along with the women and children, to plant and cultivate the fields.

Slavery in Henderson County

Slavery in Henderson County was in its early stages during the 1850s; thus it did not have a strong economic hold on the county. Yet there would be an appreciable increase in the number of slaves within the county, suggesting that slave-based agriculture was on the rise. Between 1850 and 1855, the slave population increased from 81 to 411. This represented a 407 percent increase in the number of slaves in the county. By 1860 the slave total reached 1,109, an increase of an additional 170 percent. Though the percentage of increase for the last five years of the decade is smaller than the first five years, it is still a noticeable increase.[36] The percentage of increase in the slave population, when compared to the total population of the county, far exceeded that of free inhabitants. In 1850 slaves made up about 7 percent of the county's population. By 1860 they made up 24 percent. During this same ten-year span the free population increased by about 296 percent, while the slave population increased approximately 1,269 percent. Clearly, slavery within the county was steadily gaining in importance.[37]

In a way, the county was fortunate still to be in the early stages of a slave-based economy when the Civil War started. After the war, the county's economy recovered more rapidly than many of the other southern counties which had had a larger investments in slaves. The lives of the yeoman farmers simply continued much the same as before the war. The urgency to replace a lost labor system was not as intense in Henderson County, and new ways of farming, like sharecropping, were more easily adopted.[38]

Before the war, most slaveholders in the county had been yeoman farmers owning no more than one to four slaves. Such

John Jackson Home, 1858, Jackson Chapel
— Courtesy of Henderson County Historical Commission

slaveowners maintained close personal working relationships with their slaves. Often these slaves, held by hard-working small farmers struggling to become planters, faced more difficult lives than those belonging to better-established planters. The psychological and physical pressures were greater on slaves who were under constant oversight from their masters. Slaves living on larger farms or plantations had their fellow bondsmen to turn to for identity and comfort. Slaves of the yeoman farmers in many cases had only themselves.[39]

According to the 1860 census, eighty-two of the county's 161 slaveowners owned fewer than five slaves. Some small slaveholders were in businesses outside of farming like Levi Cogburn, the potter in Athens. But the majority were yeoman farmers. These slave-owning yeoman farmers helped the area to evolve into more of a plantation society. Some yeoman farmers seem to have developed their land only to sell it later to wealthier planters. After purchasing several smaller farms, the planters merged them into single agricultural units as full-scale plantations. This process was in its initial stages at the beginning of the 1860s. Nat Coleman, the largest slave owner in the county, was a case in point. In 1860 Coleman's real estate holdings, approximately 1,416 acres, were valued at $3,400, and his personal value was $34,000. Most of his personal value came from the 50 slaves he owned. A man who owned this many slaves would not be content with only $3,400 worth of real estate. Coleman, a new arrival to the county who had not fully established himself by the time of the census, was one of four men already expanding their operations in this way.[40] Their goal, it seems, was to build on the foundations already established by yeomen farmers by buying them out.

Slavery in Henderson County had some common characteristics. First, most slaveholders were small farmers. Second, most of the slaves in the county arrived with their masters. Very few slaves were auctioned within the county, although some might have been sold at the county courthouse under terms of the probated will of a slaveowner. Third, the greatest concentration of slaves was found in the Fincastle community; more grain and other foodstuffs were produced there than any other part of the county.[41]

Slaves in Henderson County, like those in many other areas within the South, endured terrible lives. Their basic needs were met by their masters. Owners supplied them with food, shelter, and clothing. The main diet of the slaves was corn, the most commonly grown staple crop within the county. Even though the slaveowners went to great lengths to ensure their slaves' survival, they cared little about their psychological or physiological condition. An owner's need for maximum production on his farm caused him to push his slaves as much as possible. In such a world, slaves became prisoners in an economic system that could not afford to give them their freedom.[42]

The fears all Southerners shared about the institution of slavery were also present in Henderson County. Slaveholders and non-slaveholders had one major fear—the slaves might rise up against them. Such fears prepared many to overreact to rumors of slave insurrections. Anyone suspected of stirring up trouble among the slaves was kept under close surveillance.[43]

In 1860 a panic swept through Dallas, Waco, and Hender-

son, shortly after several suspicious fires were started by abolitionists and slaves. Rumors charged that two men, Antoney Wyrick and his cousin Alford Cable, living in Tennessee Colony,
Anderson County, just beyond Henderson County's southern
border, had been secretly harboring escaped slaves and also selling liquor to them. Such fears, coupled with the fact that the two
were outsiders who had lived in the area for less than three
years, created suspicions among their neighbors. People immediately began to suspect them of inciting the slaves to insurrection. The panic grew in the wake of fast spreading rumors that
northern abolitionists were encouraging slaves in other parts of
the country to burn farmhouses and poison their owners. John
Brown's failed conspiracy to unleash a general slave uprising
throughout the South beginning at Harpers Ferry, Virginia, in
October 1859 added real credibility to such rumors.[44]

The unexplained outbreak of fires throughout north and
east Texas now created even greater paranoia in Henderson
County. It has been suggested that the fires may actually have
been caused by the widespread use of a newly developed sulfur
match that could ignite on its own in intense summer heat, but
slaveholders were quick to blame northern abolitionists and
slaves.[45] Any deviation from the norm by someone in the community was cause enough to bring the individual in for ques-
tioning. When it was reported that a slave belonging to Mr. Bar-
ron, a slaveowner in the community of Science Hill, was meeting secretly with Wyrick and Cable, the decision was made to
bring all three in for an "inquiry."

The slave, named Bob, supposedly revealed during his in-
terrogation that the two men had supplied him with poison and
phosphorous and told him that the time had come for the blacks
to rise up against their masters. Bob was quickly "tried," found
guilty, and hanged. Wyrick and Cable were found later and suffered the same fate. The two men did not have to wait for their
day in court. The citizens felt no need to prolong the inevitable.[46] Whether these men were actually guilty, or not, we will
never know, but we can say that the people's fears caused an
extraordinary panic.

Slavery was not a vital part of Henderson County's economy during the 1850s. Cotton production was minimal, and large

plantations within the county were few in number. Yet even on such a small scale, slavery could have devastating effects for both slave and master. The slaveowners' fear of slave revolts stirred lurid and irrational passions. Slaves, being the most helpless and despised individuals in southern society, were often victims of imagined fears and public panic.

CHAPTER 3

Politics of Henderson County: 1846-1860

THROUGH THE EARLY part of the 1850s, Texans generally seemed committed to the well-established southern tradition
of "good-old-boy" politics. Many early elections were decided
according to a politician's popularity, personal character, and
willingness to address local needs. With the passing of each election as the decade progressed, however, the voters became increasingly aware of the broader political conflicts within their
state and nation. This awareness helped shape and direct their
political ideology in state and national affairs.

Politics in Henderson County underwent a special period of
transformation during the 1850s as the nature of its population
and its economy grew and changed. The yeoman class slowly
gave way to more prosperous prospective planters. This
changeover is clearly evident in the county toward the latter part
of the 1850s as spokesmen for the planting interest began to
advocate secession from the Union. By looking at politics from
local, state, and national levels, this transformation becomes
more understandable.

Those living in East Texas during the 1850s spoke of politics as a matter of independent personal preference, but the
truth was that voters' preferences were often influenced by local
business and social leaders. Doctors, lawyers, and planters filled

these leadership roles because their social standing within the communities demanded it.[1] A man of substance and position simply had more time to study politics and was thought to possess a greater understanding of the issues of the day. It was common for members of this class of more respectable citizens to stand as candidates for political office. Such men pursued office for a variety of reasons. O. M. Roberts suggested some were inspired by the "glamor of public life" and the "spirit of competition," others had an "ambition fed by the desire for power," and a few followed a true passion "to serve the people."[2] Although their reasons for entering politics were varied, their choice in political parties was not. Most were staunch Democrats.

Henderson County, like most of Texas, had several reasons for supporting the Democratic Party. First and foremost, the Democratic Party had endorsed Texas' efforts to enter the Union during the period of annexation.[3] Thus, the Democrats were perceived as Texas' most reliable political ally. The Democrats also increasingly championed the cause of "southern rights." Democratic support for the slaveholding interest became increasingly important to the people of Henderson County toward the close of the 1850s as slavery became more important to the county's economic future. Throughout the decade the slave population grew far more rapidly than that of whites.[4] As long as Democrats defended pro-southern positions, opposing protective tariffs and nationally funded internal improvements as well as upholding slavery, they could be assured of support in East Texas. This certainly included Henderson County.

Yet, despite overwhelming support for Democratic candidates within the county, a small element of opposition against the Democrats also persisted. The historian Randolph Campbell observes that various opposition parties in East Texas went by several names throughout the course of the 1850s: "they were Whigs in the early 1850s, Know-Nothings during the mid-decade, and Constitutional Unionists in the election of 1860."[5] The main difference between these opposition parties and the Democrats centered on disagreements over protecting southern political interests both within Texas and in the nation at large. Most "oppositionists" in Texas insisted that southern rights could best be defended by relying on constitutional law upheld in federal courts. Their views tended to be less radical than those of the pro-southern "fire-eaters" within the Democratic Party. Secession, the moderates felt, would only weaken and jeopardize the true cause of southern "rights." Yet despite their differences with the Democrats, members of the opposition still valued southern traditions. The *right* to secede they never questioned, only its practical expediency, at least until imminent danger to southern interests was seriously threatened. They were convinced that their standard of life could be best protected within the Union.[6]

The nature of the opposition vote in Henderson County is hard to pinpoint. Outside of a few specific candidates, the various opposition parties rarely attracted strong support. There were no rallies, conventions, or noted candidates within the county. It appears that those who held more conservative opinions did so with their votes alone. However, these votes seemed to suggest that not everyone thought the cause of "slavery and southern rights" demanded a continuous threat of secession.[7] The traditions and established institutions of the Union conservatives still provided ample opportunities to defend southern society's true interests.

Political leaders from both sides arose from the same well-to-do local "leadership" classes, sharing similar backgrounds and often resembling each other more than the people they represented. Such leaders normally held more wealth than the average citizen, and most were slaveholders. For the voters, politics served as an unusual source of entertainment. Citizens enjoyed gathering on the courthouse square and listening to political rhetoric aimed at winning their votes. And this was not lost on the local press. An article in the *Trinity Advocate* during the spring elections of 1858 reported "We found the candidates for District Attorney on the stump addressing the dear people for whom they entertained an abiding solicitude. Judging from the cheers and loud laughter of the sovereigns, it is but fair to presume that they were well entertained."[8] Yet the voters listened carefully to determine what personal advantages could be achieved by voting for particular candidates. This held especially true for local elections. Typically, people of the county were less interested in state and national elections because the results had less direct impact on their lives.[9]

Local politics revolved around the county's governing bodies. County elections which gained the most attention were for the offices of district and county judge, district attorney, chief justice, county clerk, sheriff, and tax assessor/collector. These positions had the greatest impact on everyday life in the county. The most influential offices were found in the courtroom.[10]

The district and county judges decided the outcomes in the county's court cases of which there were no shortages. It was important to the affluent men of the county to maintain personal influence over the individuals holding these positions. Because these prominent men often used the courts to settle lawsuits involving land and damage claims, they understood the importance of maintaining useful ties with those who could control courtroom decisions. Personal rapport with the judges might have helped in a few cases, but most judges had to be careful with their verdicts because their decisions were printed in the local newspapers and closely scrutinized by the public. Still, friendly relations with the judges could prove beneficial, especially at the county level, considering the power they possessed within the community.[11]

The role of the "chief justice," as the county's principal administrator, was particularly important. Presiding over the county commissioners' court was no small task. The chief justice monitored "the upkeep of roads, appointed slave patrols, provided for the care of indigent citizens, chose officials to handle elections, maintained necessary buildings such as the courthouse and jail, set county property taxes (within guidelines provided by the state legislature), monitored the collection of state and county taxes, and paid the salaries of public officials."[12]

County clerk, sheriff, and tax assessor/collector were positions of a more specific nature. The county clerk kept track of the property transactions within the county. The sheriff enforced state and local laws and maintained peace among the citizens. The tax assessor/collector cataloged property tax rolls and gathered taxes according to those rolls. Voters, understanding the importance of sound leadership in these offices, elected men that they believed were trustworthy.[13]

The commissioners' court itself was a vital part of county government. It was designed to promote improvements within the county by making provision for the building and maintenance of public roads, forming slave patrols to ensure protection against slave insurrections, providing care for indigent citizens, and making plans for municipal buildings. Henderson County's first commissioners' court met near the town of Buffalo on August 4, 1846. The court, lacking an official meeting hall, held the meeting in William Ware's home.[14] Their first order of business was to assign election judges for various areas within the county. Later these various areas were converted into precincts. The following precincts were arranged:

> Precinct No. 1 — southwest part of the county
> Precinct No. 2 — northwest part of the county
> Precinct No. 3 — northeast part of the county
> Precinct No. 4 — southeast part of the county[15]

The commissioners were also in charge of petitioning the federal government for new post offices. Such was the case with the 1847 term of court which sent a request to the United States postmaster general asking that Buffalo, the county seat, be given a post office. Another court responsibility was taking care of the indigent citizens of the county, in particular widows and orphaned children. Each year, money would be allotted to be spent on such cases, and the sheriff was responsible for making sure these allotments benefitted those in need.[16] The commissioners' court also played an integral part in the relocation of the county seat. Thus, the commissioners' court served the basic interests of the county's citizens in varied and immediate ways. Who held these offices was of pressing interest to all living in the county.

In the early 1850s many of the members of the commissioners' court in Henderson County were single men. Often such bachelors would live together. One example was the household of E. J. Thompson and Joshua B. Luker. Thompson served as the county clerk in 1850, and Luker, one of three men living with Thompson, was a commissioner. Both were in and out of the local political scene throughout the decade, and it is probable that they supported each other's political views during this time.

Others boarded with affluent families. Such was the case of E. M. Curtis, the chief justice in 1850. He lived with Moses Cavett who owned $3,300 worth of real estate. It is reasonable to assume that Cavett maintained some influence over Curtis. The average age of the commissioners was forty. This suggests that the voters elected men well established within the county. To be considered well established in the 1850s, however, did not require enormous wealth. The average property value held by county officials was estimated at $520, a figure which is fairly insignificant when compared with the holdings of county officials later in the decade. The officials of the earlier period also owned little personal property—a clear indication that they owned few, if any, slaves. An impressive number of these early officeholders seem to have come from Alabama. Since many people migrated from the Lower South to the East Texas area this should not be so surprising. However, it is interesting that so many of the county's politicians came from the same state.[17]

Comparing the members of the 1850 commissioners' court with those of the 1857 court shows an impressive change in their social and economic status. These changes suggest much about the direction local politics were taking in the county. First, all the members of the 1857 court appear to be married. Apparently it was now politically advantageous to be married. Politicians in the latter part of the decade also seem to have been more settled within the community and more affluent. The real estate values held by the average officeholder increased from $520 in 1850 to $1,910 in 1857. Furthermore, average personal financial worth among the commissioners increased from virtual pauper status to $3,030. Not only did these later political leaders own larger tracts of land, most by this time were also slaveholders, suggesting the emerging importance of the slaveowners' interest in the local political arena.[18]

Despite these changes, similarities continued to exist between the earlier and later groups of county leaders. The average age remained close to forty, and the majority still listed their occupations as farmers. Yet curiously their most striking similarity involved the state each of them had lived in immediately before moving to Henderson County. In almost every case this was Alabama. Perhaps this was only coincidental; yet, there is the possibility that at least some might have already known one another before coming to Texas. The appearance reinforces the perception that the county's political system was in the lines of traditional frontier "good old boy" politics.[19]

Membership in the 1860 commissioners' court seems to have continued the same pattern. There were only two major changes from 1857. First, the average age had dropped from the low forties to the upper thirties. This reduction suggests that new members in society were filling the county offices. Those who had governed the county in the early years were either dead or retired. This cleared the way for a new type of politician— younger, financially stronger, and more ambitious. One such man was Jefferson E. Thompson, the county clerk in 1861. At age twenty-eight, Thompson owned $800 in real estate and $3,100 in personal property.

The second notable change was that by the 1860s some of the commissioners clearly had achieved substantial financial security. Two such men were W. K. Faulk, uncle to Henderson County historian J. J. Faulk, and Nat P. Coleman, commissioners in the early 1860s. Faulk owned $3,200 in real estate and $19,080 in personal property. Coleman owned $3,400 in real estate and $34,500 in personal property. More than likely, such men ran for office to influence the political and economic developments of the county. As members of the planter class, they typically would have promoted the interests of an economy based on cotton production and slave labor.[20]

Evidence seems to suggest as well that the county government was changing with society. The courts, in the early part of the 1850s, had been deeply involved with the work of organizing the county. Throughout the 1850s the courts seem to have fallen under the influence of well-to-do landowners seeking personal prominence within the county. Thus it was only logical for the local government to become more closely aligned to cotton and slave interests in the county.

During the 1840s there were few statewide political issues which would have caused major concern for those living in Henderson County. For the most part, the people of the county busied themselves with local matters and took little part in state or national politics. There were certain issues, however, that did attract wide voter concern throughout Texas—frontier defense, state debt, a long-standing boundary dispute over a portion of the New Mexico Territory, and railroad development.[21]

Frontier defense in Texas was an important issue for all those living along the Trinity River. The rush of settlers coming into Texas after annexation slowly pushed the Native Americans westward. Fearing they would lose all of their lands, hard-fighting frontier tribes responded with violent attacks against encroaching settlers. Between 1836 and 1860 approximately two-hundred Texans lost their lives or were abducted during Indian raids each year.[22] In 1848 Navarro County, adjacent to Henderson County's western border, reported that Indian intrusions were causing panic among the citizens.[23] Demands grew for a stronger frontier defense. The people of Henderson County were fully aware of the frontier situation; the frontier line at this time passed just east of Waco, only some 70 miles west of the county.[24] Though no known attacks occurred in Henderson County itself between 1846 and 1860, citizens' fears strengthened support for politicians who promised to deal effectively with frontier problems.

State debt was another issue that played a part in state politics during the late 1840s. Several events had left the state in a financial crisis. Most of Texas' debt had been inherited from the Republic; however, a substantial debt had also been incurred to provide for ranger companies to patrol the frontier in order to keep the native tribes in check and supplement the United States military in the war with Mexico. It was difficult for Texas, during this time of state building, to overcome its financial troubles because of its inadequate means for raising money. The only viable resource the state owned was land, and it was giving that away to attract settlers.[25] Henderson County's interest in this issue would have been minimal. The county was mainly concerned with securing sufficient frontier defense, guaranteeing low taxes, and providing support for railroads and other internal improvements. As long as these needs were met, the people cared little about the issue of state debts.

Another major issue in Texas during this time was the controversy over Texas' western boundary claim. The state legislature insisted upon the full boundary claim established by the somewhat doubtful provisions of the Treaty of Velasco, signed by the captured Mexican President Santa Anna in 1836, which included all the regions east of the Rio Grande. This area encompassed a large portion of what was now New Mexico Territory including the long-established Hispanic settlement at Santa Fe.[26] The boundary dispute developed shortly after the Mexican War. The problem originated when American military forces, actually occupying Santa Fe, refused to accept Texas' claim to what had been recognized under Mexican rule as the separate province of New Mexico. Neither demographically nor geographically did the area show any common identity with Texas. The people of this region were primarily Hispanic; their culture and tradition made them even more defiantly determined to resist becoming part of Texas. At no time, either before or after statehood, had Texas ever actually established control over the region it claimed; throughout the whole period of the Texas Republic the area had remained firmly Mexican. Yet, despite this, President Polk, following after the annexation of Texas in 1845, had insisted on the full Rio Grande boundary claim.

During the early stages of this controversy, Governor Henderson assured the legislature that he had received confirmation from President Polk and Secretary of State James Buchanan that Texas would "retain" all it claimed. Actually this "confirmation" had been conveyed only in a letter from Buchanan, who assured the governor of his own personal support for Texas' claim but pointed out that any final decision would require action by Congress. Acting on Henderson's assurance, the Texas legislature enacted measures to create a new county in the disputed area, Santa Fe County. The purpose clearly was to consolidate Texas' claim. United States military officials, however, refused to honor Texas authority and took preliminary steps toward organizing the disputed area as part of the federal territory of New Mexico.

One of the main obstacles for Texas during this dispute was that the Democrats' control over the government had weakened. Zachary Taylor had won the presidency in 1848 as a Whig candidate. Politically, both Taylor and Vice President Millard Fillmore wanted to avoid giving Texas any portion of the New

Mexico territory. Should the area become part of Texas, it would fall under the influence of "southern interests" opposing the Whig programs of national economic activism.

Texans were enraged by the federal government's refusal to recognize Texas' perceived legal claims to the disputed area. According to the Texas legislature, the Treaty of Velasco clearly defined the Rio Grande as the southern and western boundary of their state.[27] This dispute would eventually be settled as part of the Compromise of 1850 by which Texas surrendered its claim in exchange for a ten million-dollar payment from the federal government; but until that time it remained a source for blistering rhetoric from ambitious Texas politicians, especially in gubernatorial campaigns.[28] The issue provoked much political bombast; but whether Texas voters, especially in areas like Henderson County, actually felt a stake in this issue is another matter.

By 1849 construction of railroads also became a major political issue. Railroads were viewed as vital to the future of the Texas economy. Many Texans had visions of easier access to eastern markets, lower costs for transporting their goods, and the possibility of luring new business interests into their state. Some had bigger dreams. Sam Houston introduced a resolution to the U.S. Senate on January 8, 1849, urging the feasibility of constructing a railroad running from Texas to the Pacific.[29]

During the 1840s Henderson County held little hope for railroad development because few railways had yet been projected in the East Texas region. The county's views quickly changed early in the 1850s when new state legislation was passed offering financial assistance for construction of railroads. Furthermore, plans for a private railway connecting Swanson's Landing and Marshall were already in the developmental stages.[30]

In 1849 Henderson County voted in its first gubernatorial election. The two major candidates in this race were the incumbent governor George T. Wood and former Texas Ranger Peter H. Bell. Politically speaking, both men were alike in many ways. Their main disagreements centered around the provocative but somewhat hollow boundary issue. Wood urged settling this issue through negotiations, while Bell threatened to use force to bring

Santa Fe County under Texas' jurisdiction.[31] It is doubtful that voters in Henderson County paid much attention to the candidates' opinions on this issue; the western regions of the state held little economic importance to them. As in other East Texas areas, where yeoman farmers dominated and planter influence was limited, the county's voters seldom had time to follow state politics; usually, their only guide in voting normally was a politician's personal appeal.

Wood's frontier style-of-life seemed to appeal to the voters of Henderson County because he received nearly 74 percent of their votes.[32] Another reason for Wood's success in the county was his reputation for gallant service as a colonel in command of a regiment of East Texas volunteers during the Mexican War.[33] Bell's popularity as a famous Texas Ranger mattered little when compared to enthusiasm for a local military hero. Besides, Bell was posturing as a militant southern sectionalist. During this time the more populated counties in Texas were coming more and more under planter influence. Thus Bell, a stronger advocate of the more strident strain of southern politics, won the election statewide.[34]

Texas in the early 1850s went through a number of political changes which influenced the views of citizens living in Henderson County. The boundary issue had been solved by the Compromise of 1850. Though some might not have agreed as to the benefits of the compromise, most saw it as a satisfactory solution. The most obvious reward for planters and yeoman farmers was that the state no longer had to consider paying its past debts by levying new taxes. Instead, Texas paid its debts with the money received in the settlement. As a result, concerns over the state's debts were silenced until the latter part of the decade. However, other issues including railroads and frontier defense still held significance with the voters of the county.

The county remained strong in its support of the Democratic Party throughout most of the decade, even though the Whig Party continued to retain a small following.[35] Historians suggest that the voters of Henderson County were also attracted to the Know-Nothing Party based on the county's support of D. C. Dickson, who had Know-Nothing support in the 1855 gubernatorial election. Dickson received 210 votes out of the

310 ballots cast in the county.[36] Yet Dickson's actual support within the county seems to have come from two groups, Democrats still unaware of Dickson's break with the Democratic Party and a few remaining former Whigs.[37]

The only other deviation from the Democratic Party came in the gubernatorial election of 1859 when voters in the county showed strong support for Sam Houston who ran as an independent.[38] This temporary defection from the Democratic Party in 1859 can perhaps be seen as a final stand of yeomen farmers against the planter society. Yeoman farmers, who typically owned no slaves, were more accepting of politicians like Houston who advocated using the federal government to further develop their region and state. Houston's support for using the United States military to defend the Texas frontier against Indian raids, his plans for constructing a southern route for a transcontinental railroad, and continued financial support from the United States Treasury to help pay future debts incurred by the state, were favored by the yeomen. The Democratic platform seemed to advance only the interests of slaveowners. Yet, on the national level, the yeomen tended to agree with the slaveowners' defense of the institution of slavery. After all, many yeomen farmers aspired one day to become slaveowners themselves.

In national politics, county voters supported maintaining the Union as long as the rights of slaveowners were protected by federal law, and the South held a dominant place within the American government.[39] The election of a totally sectional Republican candidate as president would be an entirely different matter. Before the Civil War, the county participated in three presidential elections. In each of these elections, voters overwhelmingly supported Democratic candidates. However, in the 1860 election, support for the Southern Democrat, John C. Breckinridge, revealed a shift toward a stronger pro-slavery stance in the political sentiments within the county at the close of the decade.[40] By this time southern extremists had skillfully gained political control in Texas and were paving the way for secession.[41]

Politically, Henderson County during the 1850s was no different than other East Texas counties. A majority of the voters throughout this time remained loyal to the Democratic Party.

Voters remained more interested in local and state issues rather than national concerns. Political candidates were often selected based upon their ability and willingness to address the needs of the county, or at least the East Texas region as a whole. Finally, even though Union sentiment was present in the county, voters were slowly swayed by the arguments of the secessionists, primarily because of their loyalty to the Democratic Party and the increasing influence of the planter class.

CHAPTER 4

Henderson County and the Secession Movement

DURING 1860, AS THE PROSPECT for a Republican presidential victory grew stronger, a wave of secession sentiment swept throughout the Lower South. Southern radicals had finally convinced Southerners that their way of life was in danger. Henderson County, like the rest of Texas, was caught up in this emotional movement fed by lurid political and social fears. Throughout the late 1850s southern extremists advocating secession from the Union marshaled strong political rhetoric, warning of dire threats at both the state and national levels, to align Texas with the Lower South and to strengthen the Democratic Party within the state.

A new breed of Democratic leaders, known for strong state's rights and secessionist views, used several political issues to promote their increasingly extremist ideology. Sam Houston, the champion of political moderation, it was argued, had betrayed the interests of Texas in 1854 when he opposed the Kansas-Nebraska Bill. Many believed Houston's vote proved that political ambitions were more important to "mere politicians of his stripe" than the interests of their constituents.[1] Southerners, especially in Texas, began to watch national politicians with a suspicious eye.

Northern refusal to accept the fugitive slave law and the activities of "fanatic" abolitionists were also cited repeatedly to frighten Southerners into accepting the extremist ideology. After 1860 most southern discussions of northern fanaticism centered around the character of John Brown, who in October 1859 had attempted to incite a violent slave revolt at Harpers Ferry, Virginia. This one incident stirred widespread paranoia throughout the South. Most Northerners, now many Southerners believed, shared in the abolitionists' desire to do away with slavery completely even by force and violence if necessary. Between 1860 and 1861 "northern abolitionists" were accused of igniting a series of mysterious fires throughout north and east Texas.[2] Furthermore, Texans charged that these "outside agitators" and incendiaries were inciting Texas slaves to rise up and kill their masters. Warnings against so called northern "conspiracies" intensified throughout East Texas. Even the town of Athens in Henderson County had exposed what many feared was a slave insurrection in its early stages of development.[3] East Texans during this time gave little leeway to any hapless "intruders" suspected of stirring up trouble among the slaves. Many of these incidents resulted in mock trials and quick death sentences for the accused.

Southern radicals within the Democratic Party were able to use such incidents to stimulate fear throughout the southern states, especially in Texas. Texans were led to believe that slavery was on the verge of extinction. Support for abolitionist activities by intruders throughout the South, it was argued, seriously threatened Texas' own agrarian-based economy.[4]

Strong loyalties to the Democratic Party were traditional for most Texans, yet faith in the Union also remained strong among many. As long as the government protected "southern rights," including what most believed the essential right to carry slavery into the newly developed territories of the West, such individuals remained unwilling to support a movement for secession.[5] Only a few "radical" unionists suggested that Texas remain part of the Union regardless of the circumstances. Almost every Texan upheld the ultimate right of an aggrieved state to secede; yet attitudes on this issue cannot be placed in two simple categories, unionist or separatist.[6]

Attitudes toward the Union actually fit into four groupings:

radical separatists, moderate separatists, moderate unionists, and radical unionists. Most Southerners rejected the extreme position on either side and embraced the more conservative "moderate" point of view. Radical separatists advocated immediate secession, charging that the government already failed to provide adequate protection of "southern rights." Radical unionists were of course the antitheses of the separatists. They remained determined never to accept secession for any reason.[7]

Most Texans stood between these two positions, believing that Texas should secede only if the government should actually threaten in some tangible way their perceived constitutional rights, particularly the right to maintain the institution of slavery. The rest fell into the category of moderate unionists, those maintaining romantic or emotional attachments to the Union. Such loyalties in many cases were to be overridden by an even deeper loyalty to Texas; after the fall of Fort Sumter many, like Sam Houston himself, would ultimately join in supporting the Confederacy.[8]

Since a majority of the county's voters gave solid support to Sam Houston in the 1859 gubernatorial election, it appeared that they fit the category of moderate unionists.[9] Yet as the secession crisis intensified in 1860, citizens in the county, like many other Texans, were persuaded by southern radicals to accept secession. By 1861 fears grew stronger throughout the entire South that the whole unique southern way of life was in jeopardy. Even non-slaveowning families, who looked to the slaveholding planter for social and economic guidance, began to feel insecure about their own future. Many, convinced that Republicans were aligned with Northern abolitionists, condemned the Republican Party without clearly understanding its actual political position. Republicans posed no direct threat to slavery where it already existed; the party platform merely condemned extending slavery any farther into the western territories.[10]

Secessionist arguments for breaking away from the United States were varied, but all insisted it was necessary in order to maintain traditional southern life. Southern extremists repeatedly cited the hallowed Kentucky and Virginia Resolutions to support their arguments for the right of secession.[11] But what was really at stake was the future of slavery. Texans were widely concerned that the newly organized free territories, positioned on their northern and western borders, might well create increasing problems over runaway slaves. Although this did not threaten slavery in Texas, it would in effect make slave labor less profitable.[12] Many also feared racial strife and warfare as a consequence of abolition. This fear, perhaps more than any other single issue, caused the majority of Southerners to join the secession movement.[13]

At this point the Southerners simply could not see how abolitionists, who opposed the very existence of slavery, differed from the vast majority of Republicans who only opposed extension of slavery into the western territories. In the panic and excitement of the moment there seemed to be little difference between the two positions. Abraham Lincoln and the "Black" Republican Party seemed an immediate threat to the very existence of the "peculiar institution."[14] Another argument for secession was based on Texas' need for close allies. Once Louisiana seceded, only Arkansas connected Texas with the United States. A sense of isolation caused many Texans to support Southern unity.[15]

Secessionists used the Democratic Party to spread their message throughout the South. Democrats in Texas did not waste any opportunity to incite the fears of their fellow citizens. Such alarmist secession rhetoric sought to align Texans with the "constitutional" Southern Democratic presidential candidate, John C. Breckinridge. The Democrats' strategy worked well, writes Walter Buenger; following Lincoln's election political leaders throughout the South found themselves "being pushed by the public to do something about the crisis believed [to be] at hand."[16] "Fire-eater" extremists now answered the people's demands with the only solution consistent with their political philosophy—secession.

As the move toward secession began to build, moderate leaders worked to keep Texas in the Union. Such "opposition" groups in Texas included Texas frontiersmen who wanted continued United States military protection against Indian raids, non-slaveholding wheat farmers in the Dallas area who saw no benefit from slavery, German immigrants who had opposed slavery ever since their arrival in Texas, former members of the

Whig Party trying to protect their dying political ideology, and state leaders, like Sam Houston and Texas Congressman Andrew Jackson Hamilton, who viewed secession itself as the true death-knell to the southern way of life. Individuals within these groups agreed that the only viable way to protect their various interests was for Texas to remain in the Union.[17] In terms of basic economic and social convictions such groups were not all that different from the secessionists. Those who opposed disunion in February 1861, wrote O. M. Roberts, "probably did so not because they opposed slavery or had other economic [or] social differences with the majority," but because "they felt that the action [secession] was too extreme for the situation."[18] History proved that leaders such as Houston and Hamilton were right in their assessments of secession.

Governor Sam Houston was perhaps the strongest opponent that southern radicals faced during their struggle to align Texas with the rest of the South. Consistent with his moderate unionist position, Houston worked diligently to keep Texas in the Union. The federal government, he insisted, could protect the rights of slaveowners far better than a group of loosely organized independent states.[19] He spoke out adamantly against southern extremists as enemies of southern rights rather than protectors. On September 22, 1860, Houston delivered a speech before a crowd at Austin in which he emphasized the need to accept Lincoln as president provided that he won the election by fair methods. Even if Lincoln were elected, Houston insisted, he could not act arbitrarily against the interests of any section; the Constitution provided safeguards against tyrants in the White House.[20] Obviously Houston was referring to the impeachment process.

In Henderson County, opponents of secession worked equally hard to preserve the Union. P. T. Tannehill, a lawyer in Athens, was the most noted advocate of unionism within the county. He was described as "an old line Whig" and "a man . . . [who] did not hesitate to reprimand or denounce wrong doing."[21] Tannehill and other unionists in the county struggled anxiously to uphold their cause, but these efforts, like those of other unionists elsewhere in Texas, did little to slow the growing spirit of secession.

Despite bold leadership, unionism began to wane in late 1860. Many considered it political heresy and did not welcome any degree of sentiment for maintaining the Union.[22] By May 1861 very few unionists remained vocal in their opposition. Public fears and anxieties now forced them either to join the secession movement, leave the country, or face the risk of outright physical violence from the highly militant secessionists. Unionists had reacted too slowly to the growing strength of the secession movement and failed to win in county elections across Texas. Thus secessionists could make it appear that a majority of Texans favored secession, especially in the Texas Secession Convention of 1861.[23]

Texas secession from the Union seemed one step closer after April 1860, when Texas walked out of the National Democratic Convention in Charleston, South Carolina. The Democratic Party now stood angrily divided over issues concerning the extension of slavery into the western territories. Northern Democrats viewed "popular sovereignty" as the answer to the slavery question, while most Southern Democrats argued against any right to exclude slavery from the territories; only a state constitution could establish or prevent slavery in any given area. Until the territories were divided into states complete with official constitutions defining their positions regarding slavery, southerners argued, all citizens retained the right to carry their slave property into any territory owned by the United States.[24] Following this split in the party, Northern Democrats nominated Stephen A. Douglas of Illinois, while the Southern Democrats chose John C. Breckinridge of Kentucky. Realistic Southerners understood the consequences of the Democratic Party's split, especially after determined moderates in the border states formed yet another southern political party, the Constitutional Union Party. Because Democratic loyalties were so bitterly divided, Lincoln, who maintained support in all of the free states except New Jersey, became the front runner.

As Lincoln's support grew and his victory became a conceivable reality, some slave owning Texans began to worry about dealing with a political party that did not receive any support from within their state. They felt sure that the Republicans, who did not support slavery, would prove hostile to Texas' social and agricultural institutions.[25] Texas Democrats played upon these fears to ensure that their state supported Breckinridge. Lincoln's election caused a panic throughout the entire South. Hysteria, a product of the southern Democratic Party's attempt to win votes, ignited the fires of secession.

This is not to say that Texans instantly embraced the arguments of the secessionists. Henderson County's state representatives in 1859, both in the Senate and in the House of Representatives, maintained a certain devotion toward the Union. Representative Anthony B. Norton, who claimed Athens as his hometown, was a strong supporter of Sam Houston and his Unionist views. Because he strongly opposed secession, Norton was forced to leave Texas in November 1861. He moved back to Mount Vernon, Ohio, his birth place, and stayed there for the next four years. In 1865 Norton returned to Texas and was elected to the Constitutional Convention of 1866 as a representative of Henderson, Kaufman, and Van Zandt counties.[26] Senator Francis M. Martin, who at the time was a resident of Corsicana in Navarro County, also opposed a break from the Union. However, unlike Norton, Martin apparently changed his mind after Texas officially seceded from the Union, because he joined the Twentieth Texas Cavalry, Company C, Confederate States Army at the outbreak of the Civil War. He served as a captain in this unit until 1862.[27]

As soon as Southern extremists in Texas received word that Lincoln had been elected, they began to call for immediate secession.[28] By the middle of November, Texas secessionists were petitioning Governor Houston to call the legislature into a special session to align Texas with the Lower South. Houston's refusal to respond prompted the secessionists to send out their own call for a public convention. The secession convention, comprised of delegates from every settled county in Texas, was to meet in January of 1861. Houston, in an attempt to slow down secession sentiment within his state, called the legislature into special session on January 21, 1861. This strategy did little to stem the growing tide of disunion. Once in session the legislature simply declared the secession convention legal, stipulating only that the move to secede would have to be voted on by the citizens of Texas.[29]

On January 28 the secession convention met as scheduled in Austin. Three days later the delegates voted to secede and declared February 23, 1861, as the date for the referendum.[30] The voters of Henderson County had elected two popular Democrats to represent the county at the secession convention, W. K. Payne and Lewis W. Moore. Payne and Moore, like most of the other delegates at the secession convention, were respected slaveowners. Each man, however, represented a different segment of society within the county. Payne, who held $250 in real estate and owned five slaves, received the support of the small farmers. Moore, on the other hand, was an upper class man. A well-known lawyer in Athens, Moore only owned one slave but held more than $2,000 in property. Despite their differences, both men carried the same message to the convention. Like the majority of Henderson County, they supported immediate secession.[31]

During the referendum, secession opponents fell silent because of threats of physical intimidation. Most unionists by this time, Buenger suggests, "decided it was foolhardy to risk offending their friends, neighbors, and business clients in opposition to something that seemed inevitable."[32] But the appearance of strong secession support in Henderson County may have been illusory. After an initial period of enthusiasm, as the war began to grind on endlessly, home front support for the Confederate cause steadily weakened. The grim reality and hardships of actual war replaced the initial assertive call to arms. Secession had come so quickly that the people did not have time to develop genuine loyalties to the Confederacy. "Secession had created unrealistic expectations and temporary unity," writes Buenger; "it did not create widespread determination to forge a southern nation at all cost."[33]

At first, citizens of Henderson County appeared to support secession enthusiastically. Before the referendum, local secessionist leaders such as William H. Martin, Rufus Dunn, and T. B. Greenwood held large meetings in the town of Athens to rally support. Few anywhere in the county openly opposed disunion, but those who did followed the leadership of Athens lawyer P. T. Tannehill. Once Texas voters approved secession, however, Tannehill and his followers remained silent.[34]

In the secession referendum, all of the counties surround-

William David Rounsavall Civil War soldier from Henderson County
— Courtesy of Henderson County Historical Commission

ing Henderson County, with the exception of Van Zandt, favored leaving the Union by at least a 6 to 1 margin.[35] Once the Civil War started, the citizens of East Texas, including those of Henderson County, stood behind Texas' decision to join the Confederacy. Few expressed disloyalty to the South.[36] Even those who did object to the war kept silent fearing that their protests might brand them as traitors, a crime punishable by death.

After Texans approved secession, the legislature immediately aligned the state with the Confederacy. For most Texans, events then moved quickly. First, a newly established public safety committee seized all of the United States military property in Texas. Soon afterward, Lieutenant Governor Edward Clark was installed to replace Sam Houston as governor, following Houston's refusal to take an oath of allegiance to the Confederacy. Finally, Texas troops were mustered to defend their new nation. Throughout the war, the citizens of Henderson County would give unselfishly to protect their southern heritage. But at the time few Texans, including those in Henderson County, could truly understand the full ramifications of secession. By the time the consequences became clear, war between the North and South had erupted with Texas inextricably committed to the fight for Confederate independence.

CHAPTER 5

Henderson County: A Typical Southern Society

Henderson County during the 1850s evolved from its original frontier condition into a more traditional southern society. During this decade the county's social structure, economics, and politics had become aligned to the patterns set by older states of the cotton South. Increasingly commercial planters had gained control over the county's original community of small independent farmers and local merchants. The Civil War brought an end to this transformation before it was fully complete, but the social and political importance of a small number of slaveowning planters living in the county before the war reveals an obvious shift in its social structure. In order to understand more clearly how Henderson County grew to resemble a "traditional" southern society by the late 1850s, it is useful to compare the county's social, economic, and political growth in this period with similar changes which occurred earlier within older areas of the South.

Henderson County's population was composed of four basic social groups: a few slaveowning commercial planters, yeoman farmers, small town craftsmen and local crossroad merchants, and slaves. The population of the county as a whole changed little during the 1850s, but the percentages that these four groups represented shifted steadily. Between 1850 and

Dennis Stewart at Tindel Farm—1940. Stewart was born into slavery in Henderson County, but was emancipated as a young child.
— Courtesy of Henderson County Historical Commission

1860 the number of slaveowners in the county increased by 700 percent, while the number of non-slaveowners decreased by approximately 42 percent.[1]

This type of social transformation was common in the South's earlier frontier regions. Each time the southern frontier moved westward, yeoman farmers were the first to settle on the new lands. Once these small farmers had developed the new region, larger farmers and slaveholding planters moved into the new territory buying up the yeomen's lands. The yeoman who sold his land often made a profit; he usually then moved farther west, bought a larger farm, perhaps even added a slave or two to his list of personal properties, and started the whole process over again.[2]

Associated with the rising number of slaveowners was a corresponding increase in the slave population. Slaves, who suffered more than any other group within the county, were helplessly placed at the bottom of the social ladder, providing all whites, especially the lowliest, a group to scorn and humiliate.

This was one aspect of a slave's life where emancipation elicited little immediate change.

Throughout the decade, yeoman farmers remained the largest white cultural group living in Henderson County. They typically planted small plots of land supporting only a single cash crop, hoping each year to make enough profit to buy provisions and equipment needed for the following planting season. Supplementing their cash crops, most also grew substantial gardens to provide their families with a stable food supply. These small farmers normally lived on their own lands in virtual isolation. In some cases, their closest neighbors might be as far as ten miles. Only a minority of yeomen owned slaves, but almost all stubbornly maintained a firm sentimental attachment to the way of life built upon slavery. As supporters of the "peculiar institution," many no doubt hoped to become slaveholders themselves.

Merchants, though few in number, remained an important part of Henderson County's society, especially in the community of Athens. Outside of Athens, in the county at large, a local merchant normally owned a single general store at some crossroads, supplying farmers of the immediate region with almost everything they needed. Other tradesmen, living in sparsely populated communities, specialized in a single area of expertise. Their commercial interests included cotton gins, grist mills, tanneries, and blacksmith shops.

Businesses in Athens, the only town of any real size, were different from those of the surrounding settlements. Here entrepreneurs capitalized on the heavier traffic coming in and out of the town. Since all local court cases were tried in Athens, the town had a greater flow of traffic than surrounding communities. However, the number of people passing through the town was minimal when compared to the traffic of small towns in more established areas. Athens also served as a convenient center for political campaigning by candidates seeking public office. On days when particularly noted politicians were scheduled to speak, the town overflowed with citizens from other areas within the county. It took little entrepreneurial sense to realize that such a frequently visited town needed hotels, retail stores, and places to eat and drink.

Henderson County's traditions in religion, education, and entertainment were aligned to those of other sparsely populated areas in the South. The religious needs of the county were chiefly taken care of by three denominations: the Baptists, Presbyterians, and Methodists. Between 1820 and 1850 each of these religious groups, especially the Baptists and Methodists, experienced steady growth throughout the South as a whole. During this period Methodists in Virginia, North and South Carolina, and Georgia gained 130,713 new members, and Baptists in the same four states increased by nearly 150,000.[3]

Despite crude conditions, the people of Henderson County, like most Southerners, were genuinely committed to educating their children. School houses were usually simple one-room structures. One teacher normally taught a class of ten to thirty students. The students varied both in age and academic abilities. Such conditions were not the most favorable for learning but were common throughout southern frontier regions.[4]

Henderson County enjoyed many typical southern frontier entertainments. Aside from drinking, gambling, and horse racing, the citizens of the county entertained themselves by reading newspapers and books, attending social gatherings on Saturday and Sunday afternoons, and occasionally listening to a politician's charismatic campaign speech during election times. Politics, serving as a favorite spectator sport, provided all classes of Southerners with a brief escape from ordinary daily routines.[5]

Economic conditions, on which all else rested, also paralleled those generally found in the South. Agriculture was the main source of income within the county. Wheat had been the primary crop grown by the earliest settlers, but this slowly gave way to a more profitable crop—cotton. "King Cotton" seemed preferential to wheat because it brought a higher price and maintained well-established markets. Henderson County produced less cotton than other more developed cotton producing areas in Texas, but the county did show a steady increase in production between 1850 and 1860. Possibly, if the Civil War had not interrupted this economic trend, the county might have become a major cotton producing area in East Texas.[6]

Farmers, aside from growing cash crops, raised various types of livestock, especially cattle and hogs. These provided additional income from meat and hides. As on most frontier farms, the animals roamed the areas surrounding the farmers' lands.[7]

During the 1850s slavery slowly gained economic importance in Henderson County. Slaves accounted for 20 to 30 percent of the county's growing population. As the number of slaves increased, free citizens living in the county grew increasingly attached to the idea of slavery. By 1860 everyone in the county was keenly aware of the rewards, fears, and hardships associated with the "peculiar institution."

The benefits of slavery seemed clear to most southern farmers. Slavery not only offered slaveowners a tangible measure of social status, because of the substantial investment needed to purchase slaves, but also solved basic labor problems especially in the southern frontier regions where free workers enjoyed many other, more attractive, opportunities. Slavery provided a perpetual labor system; the farmer who owned slaves did not have to worry about hired workers seeking better opportunities after only one or two growing seasons.[8] Yet slavery also created certain fears among white Southerners living in areas heavily populated with slaves.

Such fears can be traced back as far as the Stono rebellion in South Carolina in 1739 and the slave insurrection in the French West Indies colony of Santo Domingo in 1791. Southern alarm over the influence of abolitionists was especially fueled by memories of the Santo Domingo uprising. Latin American and United States slaveowners alike firmly believed that radical French abolitionists, known as the *Amis des Noirs* or Friends of the Blacks, had been actively responsible for the revolt in Santo Domingo.[9] As a result, Southerners incessantly rejected even the mildest criticisms of slavery fearing the possibility of similar slave uprisings in their own communities. Believing as they did that the Santo Domingo revolt had been started by infiltrators posing as ordinary citizens of the colony, they were beset by mounting "fears of being infiltrated, of being secretly penetrated, seized and overthrown at one's most vulnerable point."[10] Following the Santo Domingo revolt, throughout the early 1800s southern fears seemed comfirmed by later slave conspiracies much closer to home, especially the abortive Gabriel Prosser plot in 1800 at Richmond, Virginia, the Denmark Vesey conspiracy of 1822 in Charleston, South Carolina, and the bloody Nat Turner uprising of 1831 in Southhampton County, Virginia.[11]

Fears like these drove Southerners, including those living in Henderson County, to overreact to situations like the intense sectional controversy over the Kansas-Nebraska Act during the mid 1850s and John Brown's raid on Harpers Ferry, Virginia, in 1859. Some imagined the struggle over Kansas as an abolitionist plot to set up a base to infiltrate the recently settled slave states of Missouri, Arkansas, and Texas. The loss of Kansas, it was believed, would inevitably lead to the loss of Missouri. "From such a base, underground railroads might diverge to every city, town, and plantation, leading to insurrection and a war [against slaveowners]."[12] There were few limits to the lurid forms such fears might take.

As the decade progressed, the citizens of Henderson County were caught up in this frantic and paranoid style of thinking, especially during the period of the famous Texas fires at the peak of the secession crisis when a violent mob killed three men from the southwestern part of the county suspected of being involved in a conspiracy against the community of Science Hill.[13] Historian David Davis describes such conspiracy panics starkly: ". . . the tactics of lynch law were soon reduced to a deliberate system of terrorism, in which solid citizens would take the lead, pretending to uphold law and order, only to give free rein to hired thugs and drunken rabble who would carry mob violence to its predictable extremes."[14] The situation in Henderson County could not be described more aptly.

It was politics where Henderson County most resembled the rest of the South.[15] As in most counties throughout the South, Henderson County's political leaders came from among its more prominent citizens. Most all these men owned slaves, and their livelihoods tended to fall into two distinct occupations, either as farmers or lawyers. This is not surprising considering that these were the most commonly found occupations along the southern frontier.

The Democratic Party was especially popular in Henderson County. Such loyalties stemmed primarily from the Democrats role in promoting Texas annexation in 1845. The party spoke for maintaining southern traditions, which to most people simply meant preserving slavery and the whole way of life that rested on it. Such an appeal clearly attracted slaveowners, but it also captivated those who hoped to own slaves in the future. This included most white Southerners.

Aside from sectional concerns, two political issues in particular were shared both in Henderson County and other parts of the frontier South—defense against Indians and railroad development. Fear of Indians was already a well established feature of southern tradition. Since the beginning of the colonial period, Indian raids had made the southern frontier a dangerous place. The Texas frontier during the antebellum period was no different. Though the people of Henderson County by the 1850s were basically shielded from Indian raids, they had friends and family living less than 150 miles away who experienced frequent encounters with hostile tribes. Thus, the county maintained a strong interest in supporting protection of the frontier by both state and national governments.

The need for railroad development was also an important political theme in the county. Railroads provided a faster and more efficient means to carry crops to market. Without cheap and effective bulk transportation, commercial farming of staple crops was impossible. The creation of new railroad lines, allowing crops to be shipped by trains instead of wagons, enabled southern farmers like those living in Henderson County to produce larger quantities of crops for eastern markets. As a result, the quality of life improved along with rising yearly earnings.

Toward the end of the 1850s secession sentiment ran high throughout the entire South. Henderson County, like much of the South, was swept up by the appeal of this movement. Fears of an abolitionist plot to destroy the southern economy caused many citizens to act irrationally. Some of them called for immediate secession. Many, however, while supporting the idea of secession, urged greater caution.

Southerners wanted to protect their traditional way of life, especially the institution of slavery which to many seemed seriously threatened. Southerners were deeply concerned over the future of the country, especially after a sectional presidential

Sheriff K. Richardson Civil War Veteran.
— Courtesy of Henderson County Historical Commission

candidate, Abraham Lincoln, had been elected president. Such a president, it was widely believed, would surely destroy the long-standing central institution of the South, slavery. Northern Republicans and abolitionists alike were viewed as having little or no regard for constitutional law, at least as Southerners interpreted it. Following the Republican victory, extremists argued, it would only be a matter of time before the country fell under the influence of a "lawless rabble."

Secession was strongly supported within Henderson County by 1861, but some of the county's more conservative citizens still advocated tentative Unionism. Unionists like these were also common throughout the South, and their presence in Henderson County reveals once again how the county closely fit the common pattern in southern society.[16] Ultimately, despite the misgivings of a small but determined contingent of Unionists, the county was swept by the secessionist cause.

Initial support for the war can be gauged by the militia muster roles for the county. Just as in most areas throughout the South, Henderson County's men and boys rushed to join local volunteer companies. Their minds were full of heroic battle scenes, parades given in honor of great victories, a sweetheart's admiration and love for the one who fought to uphold southern honor and traditions. Many recruits also visualized themselves as patriots and respected military heroes. Few, if any, realized the overwhelming devastation they were about to face in one of America's most brutal wars.[17]

The Civil War created many hardships for this small East Texas county, even though no actual battles took place here. The war's impact can be measured by the number of men leaving the county to fight in distant battles. Their wives, sons, and daughters were left behind to maintain stores, shops, and family farms. Though women were no strangers to hard work, they now had to take on the additional burden of running the family business. A job they often handled with a remarkable degree of success. Despite their efforts however, by the end of the war most farms were operating on a subsistence level; a situation primarily attributable to the war's drain on the southern economy.

After 1865, Reconstruction provided new obstacles to the already devastated southern economy. Henderson County's social structure, labor system, and government all went through dramatic changes. In every case the traditional southern principles that the county had embraced during the 1850s proved to be futile in dealing with the new problems of Reconstruction. Henderson County, like many areas within East Texas, had to overcome old fears regarding the former slaves and accept a new, slaveless society. Most were able to cope with the changes, but the Reconstruction years would be a new time of tension and social stalemate. Only after this period of adjustment had passed would Henderson County show any significant signs of renewed advancement.

CHAPTER 6

Early Settlers of Henderson County

IN ORDER FOR THIS study to be complete, it was necessary
to examine the lives of the citizens who lived in Henderson
County prior to the outbreak of the American Civil War. Therefore, the author has compiled a series of brief biographical
sketches of a few select individuals who lived in the county during the antebellum period.

Most of the information in this chapter was located in the
"Old Settlers Edition" of the *Athens Review* printed August 2,
1901.[1] This edition contains over thirty short biographies of
individuals who settled in the county during its formative period. When it was possible, the information found in the "Old
Settlers Edition" was cross-referenced with J. J. Faulk's *History of
Henderson County* to check for inconsistencies. In addition, the
biographical sketches were reviewed by two local historians of
Henderson County: Frank La Rue, Jr., currently the chairman
of the Henderson County Historical Commission, and Art Hall,
a past chairman of the Henderson County Historical Commission. Because a great deal of the information in this chapter
comes from the "Old Settlers Edition" of the *Athens Review*, the
use of footnotes in this chapter has been curtailed.

Although the biographical information that follows is somewhat limited in scope, it will offer the reader a clearer picture of

the human character present in the county between 1846 and 1860. As one reads the sketches of the early citizens of Henderson County, it becomes evident that these people lived in a world very different from our own. It was a wild, untamed, and harsh period in the county's history. Yet, at the same time, the county had a certain "Garden of Eden" character to it. In other words, the early settlers found themselves living in a heavenly hell.

Most of the women who moved to Henderson County during its early period followed their husbands or fathers. The men came to the county with intentions of carving out a new and more fruitful existence from the fertile fields present there. Some early pioneers stayed in the area for the remainder of their lives; others moved on seeking greater opportunities elsewhere.

Mrs. Dull Avriett

Dull Avriett was born in 1834 at Maringo County, Alabama. She, along with her mother and three brothers, arrived in Henderson County on November 22, 1847. Mrs. Avriett recalled that her family's original intent was to settle to the north of the county, but, like so many of the migrant travelers

Mrs. Dull Avriett
— Courtesy of Henderson
County Historical
Commission

who braved the winter storms of Texas, they were forced to change their direction of travel southward due to an unrelenting blue norther. Mrs. Avriett's family took refuge from the bitter winter storm at Samuel Whitehead's campsite located on Caney Creek. Sometime during their stay, Charles Mercer, who at that time was trying to find settlers for his thinly populated Mercer Colony, visited the camp and offered each family member present a certificate for land located within his colony. As fate would have it, these certificates were for lands situated in Henderson County. Mrs. Avriett recalled that Samuel Whitehead, Asa Dalton, Billy Daniels, Mr. Fancher, and W. W. Loop were already living in the county at the time of her family's arrival.

Mrs. Avriett's mother died in 1855. Although her mother's life was short-lived in the county, she did manage to become one of the first women to marry inside the borders of Henderson County. Her spouse, one of the county's more prominent men, was John "Red" Brown.

Mrs. Avriett is credited by state and local historians as the woman who actually named the city of Athens. Apparently, she suggested the name to her step-father, John Brown, who liked the name so well that he presented it before the commissioners' court for approval. Because of his influence, and owing to the fact that few were willing to put too much thought to the matter, Athens was selected as name of the newly established settlement.

In 1851 Mrs. Avriett herself was married to a prominent county figure, E. J. Thompson. After their wedding, the couple quickly moved to Athens and began to establish themselves as a principal force in developing the newly formed town. Mrs. Avriett recalled that Athens was thinly populated when she and her husband first arrived. At that time the only people living in "town" or nearby were Joab McManus, E. A. Carroll, C. B. Meredith, Mrs. Racina Clark, and Miss Jurusha Ingram. Mrs. Avriett also asserted that Ida Butcher was the first child born in Athens. According to 1860 Census Records for Henderson County, this birth would have taken place sometime in 1853.

Prior to the Civil War, E. J. Thompson and his wife built one of the earlier hotels located in Athens. It was opened for business in May of 1860 and quickly gained favor with the town's socialites. In the fall of 1860 the hotel was the site of a big secession ball.

The Civil War brought heartache and misery to Mrs. Avriett's life. Her husband died just four weeks after enlisting in the Confederate Army in 1861. Though Mrs. Avriett did not mention the cause of her spouse's death, it is reasonable to assume that he died of some type of infectious disease—a common cause of death among soldiers during the war.

Mrs. Emma D. Carroll (Butcher)

Mrs. Emma D. Carroll
— Courtesy of *Athens Daily Review*

Mrs. Emmarine D. Butcher was born December 15, 1834, in the state of Kentucky. In 1852 she was married to E. A. Carroll, a well-known man in the early history of the county. Between 1852 and 1860, Mr. Carroll served twice as sheriff of Henderson County and once as a county commissioner. Mrs. Carroll obviously possessed a strong mental and physical constitution. Between 1860 and the time of her death in 1901, Mrs. Carroll witnessed the burial of her husband and four of her eight children.

Nat P. Coleman

N. P. Coleman was born June 9, 1823, in Clark County, Alabama. He moved to Henderson County in 1853. Coleman was a deeply religious man. Throughout his life, he remained a faithful member of the Cumberland Presbyterian Church. Coleman was also a very successful businessman and undoubtedly one of the richest men in the county during the 1850s. He was a loyal member of the Masonic Order and spent much of his time devoted to Masonic projects, such as addressing the educational needs of the county. Many Confederate veterans from Henderson County remembered Coleman's unselfish efforts during the Civil War. Although he did not join the Confederate army, he did give supplies and assistance to the families of those men

Nat P. Coleman
— Courtesy of *Athens Daily Review*

in the county who did enlist. When these soldiers went to the battlefields, they could at least take some comfort in the fact that men like Coleman were watching over their families.

At the end of the war, Coleman was forced to free some seventy-seven slaves. This alone left him in near financial ruin. However, due to his strong character, good business judgement, and large landholdings, he was able to recover from the devastation of the Civil War and Reconstruction.

Mrs. Gerryid Easterling

Mrs. Gerryid Easterling
— Courtesy of *Athens Daily Review*

Mrs. Gerryid Meredith came to Henderson County with her first husband, C. B. Meredith. The couple arrived in Henderson County in September 1851. Mrs. Meredith remembered that the first courthouse in Athens was a simple log cabin. Mr. Meredith and E. A. Carroll built the first store house in Athens. The building was made by setting poles in the ground and nailing red oak boards on the outside to form the walls. For a period of time, the building stood without a solid door. The proprietors simply hung an old blanket in the entrance. Mr. Meredith died in the late 1850s. Soon afterward, Mrs. Gerryid Meredith, desiring the comfort and aid of friends and family, decided to move back to her home state of Georgia. During her return to Georgia, Mrs. Meredith married a prominent Georgian, Judge J. N. Easterling.

Judge James J. Faulk

During the 1850s Judge Faulk was a young boy living in the Fincastle community with his family. Mr. Faulk was born February 11, 1851, in Ouachita Parish, Louisiana. In 1929 he wrote

Judge James J. Faulk
— Courtesy of *Athens Daily Review*

the *History of Henderson County*, which was based upon his personal experiences as well as those of other citizens living in the county. His book remains one of the best written accounts of the county's early history and is often cited by modern scholars.

John W. Fulton

John W. Fulton was born in 1823 in Knox County, Tennessee. Having moved to Henderson County in 1848, he had the opportunity to participate in the election that determined the final location of the county seat of government. Fulton recalled the 1850s as the "grand old happy days." He remembered that the men in the county would meet once or twice a year to attend the district court. Apparently, jury duty was considered as much a social gathering as it was a civic responsibility. He reminisced that occasionally two bullies would meet and have a fist fight, the winner putting an end to all ill feeling. Fulton enlisted late in the war in what was known at first as the Captain James Avriett Company, and afterwards, the Captain W. K. Payne Company. It is written that Mr. Fulton made a good soldier.

Hon. William H. Graham

In 1838 W. H. Graham was born in Raleigh, Smith County, Mississippi. He moved to Henderson County in 1856. When the Civil War broke out, he quickly joined the Confederate Army. Graham was present at the fall of Arkansas Post and taken pris-

oner. Before being sent to Richmond, Virginia, as part of a pris-
oner exchange program, Graham spent several months in a
prison camp located in Chicago. At Richmond, Graham and
other prisoners of war were released to the Confederate army in
exchange for captured Union troops—a customary practice during the early part of the war. After his release, Graham served
with the Army of Tennessee until its surrender at Greensbor-
ough, North Carolina.

Reverend Robert Hodge

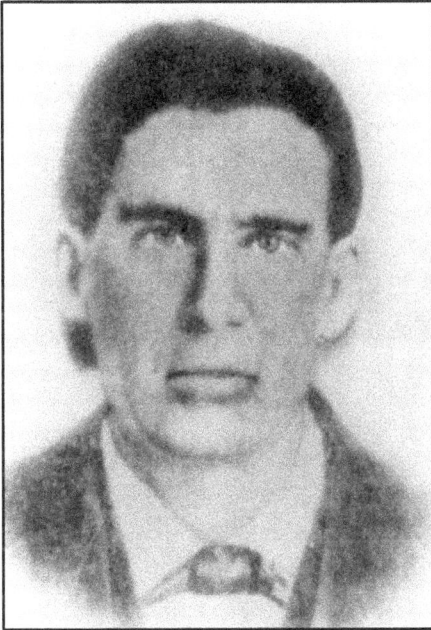

Rev. Robert H. Hodge
— Courtesy of Henderson County
Historical Commission

Reverend Robert
Hodge was born in Tennes-
see in 1805. He moved to
Mississippi in 1823. While
living in Mississippi, he
married Miss Miliscent B.
Hall, a niece of Hiram G.
Runnels who was governor
of Mississippi from 1833 to
1835. Miliscent was also
cousin to Hardin R. "Dick"
Runnels, who was the gov-
ernor of Texas from 1857
to 1859. Hodge moved to
Texas in 1850, first settling
in Anderson County near
Old Brushy Creek. In the
spring of 1852 he moved to
Henderson County, settling in the Science Hill community. It
was recorded that he was a leading organizer of the Science Hill
Academy. Throughout his life, Hodge remained a devoted
Cumberland Presbyterian minister with the goal of winning
souls firmly etched upon his heart. Reverend Hodge was a well
respected man in his day and was afforded the privilege of
preaching in many of the county's churches before and during
the Civil War.

James A. Knight

On September 22, 1833, James A. Knight was born in the state of Alabama. He moved to Henderson County in 1849. Soon after arriving in the county, Knight entered successfully into the agricultural business. In 1861 he enlisted in the Confederate army and served until the end of the war.

Dr. William C. Larkin

Dr. William C. Larkin was born June 1832 in the state of Tennessee. He spent his childhood years on a farm along the Tennessee-Alabama state line. Unlike many of his peers, Larkin was fortunate enough to obtain a

Dr. W. C. Larkin
— Courtesy of *Athens Daily Review*

thorough education. After receiving his literacy education in Lebanon, Tennessee, he began attending classes in 1858 at the University of Pennsylvania. Larkin graduated with honors from the university, receiving a degree in medicine.

Larkin moved to Henderson County, settling near Athens, sometime in late 1859 or early 1860. When the secession crisis became an issue in Texas, he firmly took the side of the secessionists. At the time, Larkin owned approximately $8,000 in slave property.

During the Civil War Larkin stayed at home. Though he did not go into battle, Larkin did much to help ease the minds of the soldiers from this county. While the enlisted men were fighting on distant battlefields, Dr. Larkin was back home taking care of their families' medical needs.

Joseph M. La Rue

Joseph M. La Rue was born June 20, 1825, in Bedford County, Tennessee. In 1853 Mr. La Rue, accompanied by his

Joseph M. La Rue and Mary Frances Oliver La Rue
— Courtesy of Henderson County Historical Commission

La Rue-Hardin Home, 1858, Unity
— Courtesy of Henderson County Commission

brother Isaac, moved to Henderson County. They settled an area approximately ten miles northeast of Athens. Upon his arrival, Joseph La Rue actively engaged in farming and stock raising.

Despite the fact that he owned a slave, La Rue, during the secession crisis, strongly opposed breaking away from the Union. Like Sam Houston and other men of thought, he urged a more conservative approach to the problem of how to protect "southern rights." When the county voted on the matter in the state referendum, however, La Rue voted in favor of secession. Apparently, pressure from close friends, such as Dr. Mabry and James Avriett, caused La Rue to change his mind.

Once La Rue had changed his mind, he did not hesitate to fully support his decision. He joined the Confederate army and served under Captain Jerry Warren in Company F, 20th Texas Cavalry in the Trans-Mississippi Department in Colonel Bass' Regiment.

Major William Harrison "Howdy" Martin[2]

William H. Martin, referred to by his friends simply as Bill Martin, is undoubtedly one of the better-known individuals from the early period in Henderson County. His military service alone gives him distinction. He led troops in some of the bloodiest battles fought during the Civil War: Chickamauga, Gaines' Mill, and Gettysburg. Martin was not, however, a career military man.

William Harrison "Howdy" Martin
— Courtesy of Henderson County Commission

W. H. Martin was born on May 23, 1823, at Barbour County, Alabama. As a young man, he studied law for several weeks at Troy, Alabama, and was admitted to the Alabama bar. Martin left Alabama and came to Texas in 1850. Within two years of his arrival, he was able to obtain a modest reputation as a lawyer. It was during this time that he bought a house in Athens. In 1853 Martin, a "state's rights" Democrat, was elected to serve in the Texas Senate—a position he held until 1857.

When the Civil War broke out, Martin recruited a company of men from Henderson County to serve in the Confederate army. Martin's men officially formed Company K of the Texas Fourth Infantry Regiment. Captain Martin would lead his men for nearly four years before being promoted to the rank of major. Before the surrender at Appomatox, he was brevetted a lieutenant colonel.

It was during the war that Martin received his nickname, "Old Howdy." Apparently, his men gave him the moniker because Martin always tipped his fingers to his hat brim and said "howdy" rather than saluting. Martin and his men fought in many battles during the war including Eltham's Landing, Seven Pines, Gaines' Mill, Second Manassas, Sharpsburg, Chancellorsville, Gettysburg, the Wilderness, Spotsylvania, Cold Harbor, Petersburg, and wherever else the Army of Northern Virginia fought.

It was recorded that Martin carried two rather large pistols, affectionately referred to by his men as "Martin's Batteries." Apparently, Martin would pull out his pistols during the course of a battle and begin firing shots at the enemy. Each time Martin fired one of his his sidearms, he would pause and bark out another command to his men. After the war, one Confederate veteran recalled "Martin would lead a charge while making a 4th of July type speech." As he advanced, Martin would yell to his men "Your wives and your children" and "Your homes and your firesides."

Although Martin was a brave leader, he lacked the stern discipline of a good commander. This could explain why four years passed before Martin was promoted in rank. Martin was viewed by his superiors, like John Bell Hood, as a commander who cared too much for his men to be a good military leader. For example, when the boys in Company K would go into town and get drunk on Virginia applejack, raise hell, and wind up in jail, they would send for Martin who in most cases would only give the men a stiff warning.

Joab McManus

Joab McManus was born June 24, 1817, in Murray County, Tennessee. When he was thirteen years old, he and his father moved to Sangamon, Illinois, where he reportedly became a personal acquaintance of Abraham Lincoln. After several more moves throughout the South, McManus, along with W. W. Stirman, W. B. Stirman, and Mrs. Butcher, came to Henderson

Joab McManus
—Courtesy of *Athens Daily Review*

County in 1848. Shortly after his arrival, McManus was elected justice of the peace of Henderson County. In 1850 he was elected as a commissioner of the county, and later he served as the county treasurer. McManus was involved in many of the early political decisions of Henderson County, and his judgement was well respected by the county's early citizens.

James A. Mitcham

James A. Mitcham was born in 1822 at Clark County, Alabama. He moved to Texas in 1846 settling in Anderson County. In 1850 he moved to Henderson County making his home on Caney Creek, six miles west of Athens.

Mitcham, like many men in the county, was an active member in the Masonic Order. Religiously, he was an ardent Methodist. Politically, he was described as an "Old Line Whig." Mitcham, a great admirer of Sam Houston, was strongly opposed to secession. Obviously, like Houston, he felt that "southern rights" could be better supported by the principles established in the United States Constitution.

Col. T. F. Murchison

T. F. Murchison was born February 9, 1828, in Marshall County, Mississippi. He moved to Henderson County on June 29, 1855. Upon his arrival, Murchison found work selling goods in Dr. Collins mercantile store. By 1859 Murchison had acquired the necessary capital to open his own mercantile business in Athens.

When the war between the states broke out, Murchison and Captain Warren raised a cavalry company for service in the Confederate army. This

Col. T. F. Murchison
— Courtesy of Athens Daily Review

company was later dismounted and Murchison returned home. Apparently, like many Texans during the war, he had no desire to serve in an infantry unit. Though Murchison never served in the field, he remained mustered in the service throughout the war at the rank and pay of captain. During this time, he served as the "Enlistment Officer" for Henderson County.

J. M. Pickens

J. M. Pickens was born in the state of Alabama sometime in 1828. After moving to Henderson County in 1857, he established himself as a very successful farmer. It is recorded that he was a man of sterling integrity, persistent industry, and deep religious conviction. During the war Pickens served as a "Patty

Roller." This was a person who in the evening traveled over a designated area making sure the slaves were in their quarters at the end of the workday.

Mrs. Lucy A. Royall (Walton)

Mrs. Lucy A. Royall
— Courtesy of *Athens Daily Review*

Lucy A. Royall, whose maiden name was Walton, was born on August 17, 1814, in Pittsylvania County, Virginia. She was married on November 25, 1835, to another native Virginian, John Royall. The Royalls moved to Texas in November of 1853 and arrived in Athens during the latter part of December. They chose to settle an area two miles to the east of Athens. By 1860 the couple had achieved a measurable degree of success—owning approximately 800 acres of land and one slave.

Henry C. Tindell

Henry C. Tindell was born in the state of Alabama sometime in 1844. He moved to Henderson County with his family in 1852 settling with them near the Fincastle community. As a boy growing up, Tindell became a marksman with a rifle. It was recorded that he used his talents with a rifle to win several

shooting matches held in the Fincastle area. William K. Faulk also remembered that Tindell was very handy with a whip. According to Faulk, he was the only boy who could pop a whip twice, once in front of his position and then once behind, without wrapping it around his neck.

When he was just eighteen year old, Tindell joined the Confederate army. When his position at Arkansas Post was overrun with Federal troops, he was able to escape capture. Tindell soon afterwards joined the 17th Consolidated Regiment and fought with them on the Red River at Harrisonburg. During the battle at Harrisonburg, a shell from a gunboat swept Tindell's hair and hide from the top of his head. After sustaining this near fatal injury, he was furloughed home to recover. Tindell was somewhat fortunate in being sent home, because he missed two of the more

Adams-Tindel Home, 1851, (Fincastle)
— Courtesy of Henderson County Historical Commission

bloody engagements fought west of the Red River—the battles of Pleasant Hill and Mansfield.

Mrs. Jurusha Walker (Ingram)

Mrs. Jerusha Walker
— Courtesy of *Athens Daily Review*

Miss Jurusha Ingram was born June 22, 1836, in Sumpter County, Alabama. When she was two years old, her mother died leaving the young girl in the care of her uncle, E. J. Thompson. The two oddly paired travelers moved to Texas in 1845. They first settled in Panola County before moving to Henderson County three years later. In 1850 they moved to Athens. Mrs. Ingram recalled the day when she first arrived in Athens; conditions in the newly created town were crude at best. As she recalled, the only building in town at that time was a log cabin—the home and office of the county clerk. Considering this was the only erected structure in town, Thompson and his niece temporarily moved into this cabin the morning of their arrival. Later that same day, Joab McManus and his family also moved into the cabin. Though conditions were cramped and rudimentary, Mrs. Ingram, later in her life, took pride in the fact that she was the first female ever to live in the town of Athens. In February 1859 Miss Ingram was married to William D. Walker, who was a contractor from Georgia. Mr. Walker was the contractor responsible for building the Deen Hotel, which housed the visitors of Athens for many years.

B. W. J. "Bush" Wofford

B. W. J. Wofford was born February 27, 1832, in Huntsville, Alabama. He moved to Henderson County in the spring of 1851 settling near the Fincastle community. Upon arriving in the county, he successfully engaged in mercantile, farming, and stockraising buisnesses. By 1860 Wofford held twenty-five slaves and 1,300 acres of land.

B. W. J. Wofford
— Courtesy of *Athens Daily Review*

W. H. (Bose) Coleman Home, 1857,
southeast of Athens/Old Pine Grove Road
— Courtesy of Henderson County Historical Commission

APPENDIX ONE

Prominent Citizens of the Buffalo Community

The following is a membership list of the Buffalo Lyceum. These names were taken from J. J. Faulk's *History of Henderson County*, pages 14-15. These men owned land in either Buffalo or nearby areas. It seems clear that these men had high aspirations to turn their lands into a miniture cotton empire, especially considering one of the questions pondered by the members of the Buffalo Lyceum was how to make the Trinity River more navigable, thus making it more practical to send their bales of cotton to markets on the lower end of the river.

Henry Jefferys
A. M. Moore
James Stephenson
J. D. Scott
J. S. Boggs
J. T. Royal
W. R. Hughes
Sam Jones
Jason McCane
Jason Williamson
Samuel Kirk
Z. W. Moore
H. Moore

John H. Reagan
A. B. Gorden
F. M. Scott
P. T. Bufford
B. Gains
James Duncan
L. B. Sanders
Jason McCane
Nelson Cogburn
F. L. Brown
R. V. Carlisle
Peter Hill

APPENDIX TWO

Local Politicians of Henderson County, 1846-1860

Chief Justice:

John Damron
B. Graham
M. C. Howard
E. M. Curtis
Joshua B. Luker
Samuel Owen
D. A. Owen

County Clerk:

Albert Kimbell
James Boggs
L. B. Hart
J. T. Royal
E. J. Thompson
James Trimble
John Trimble
William Gray
Jere Warren
J. M. Sterman

Sheriff:

B. Shankle
J. B. Davenport

William Gray
James Ball
W. C. Bobo
A. J. McDonald
E. A. Carroll
Tandy Howeth
Jess Smith

Commissioners:

R. R. Powers
R. W. Kyle
P. T. Bufford
J. S. Trimble
W. F. Clark
K. K. Knight
W. R. Clark
Tom Berry
Sam Richardson
W. W. Carver
J. A. Goodgame
William Peters
James A. Nordain
Peter Hill
William H. McBee
William Ware
David Carlisle

Alfred Moore
Thacker Vivion, Sr.
James Hooker
J. Stephenson
Sterling R. Barnes
L. D. Stover
John Spikes
N. T. Dickerson
Victor Pannell
John "Red" Brown
John S. Ledbetter
Joshua B. Luker
Durham Avant
John N. Sullivan
Thomas Kelm
Joab McManus
J. A. Mitcham
N. P. Coleman
A. M. Cobb
Tandy Howeth
W. K. Faulk
R. H. Pearson
J. G. Ratcliff
A. J. Laymance
William Hogg
John G. Dunn
E. A. Carroll

APPENDIX THREE

Muster Rolls for Henderson County

The following muster rolls of companies raised in Henderson County were taken from Leila Reeves Eads' *Defenders: A Confederate History of Henderson County, Texas*. Some first and middle names were reduced to their initials to save space. Also, some of the names appear on more than one enlistment sheet.

From the microfilm record Number 586 in the Texas State Archives. A group of volunteers from Henderson County who joined the Confederate Army after the Confederate States of America requested the service of five thousand men. These men later became part of Hood's Texas Brigade, Company K, 4th Texas Infantry Regiment. The group left Athens July 21, 1861.

Officers:
W. H. Martin, Capt.; John F. Wilson, 1st Lt.; John K. Richardson, 2nd Lt.; D. M. Marbry, 3rd Lt.; L. B. Thomas, 1st Sgt.; Samuel F. Owens, 2nd Sgt.; Henry Martin, 3rd Sgt.; John R. McGill, 4th Sgt.; James Palmer, 1st Cpl.; John Bethel, 2nd Cpl.; D. M. Rushing, 3rd Cpl.; R. W. Jordan, 4th Cpl.

Privates:
Tandy Howeth, E. J. Thompson, Rufus S. Dunn, Thm. B. Greenwood, David Bellows, H. La Rue, J. J. Parker, M. C. Clanahan, James M. Bass, K. M. Bass, K. M. Ratcliff, W. C. Holland, James Swindle, K. Richardson, W. J. Murchison, W. H. Sullivan, S. T. Owen, J. T. Burriss, John Adams, James E. Beall, F. J. Smith, J. F. Matthews, T. M. Banks, John E. Beall, Joseph Loop, Joseph Green, Jethro Campbell, H. M. Morrison, Robert Martin, A. Coleman, W. J. Morrison, W. K. Matthews, M. Mills, Matt Walker, W. K. Paine, Hugh Carter, John McDonald, James Green, R. A. Bethel, T. M. Webb, W. Dalton, J. K. La Rue, Lewis M. Moore, F. Hobgood, W. B. Owens, W. S. Dalton, John Clark, G. W. Boman, W. M. Tucker, Andy Campbell, L. J. Gutherie, J. D. Heard, J. H. Murdock, John Lisco, D. A. Carriffee, John Carroll, Wm. Spears, A. Campbell, J. F. Matthews, Andy Mitchell, Saul Rogers, Joseph Rhodes, Crib Choat, Wm. Richardson, M. J. O'Neal, J. W. Franks, W. H. Gee, J. D. Owen, James Sullivan, Robert B. Paul, John Rounsavall, J. Y. McManus, G. W. Nichols, W. G. Middleton, Isaac C. Mills, L. Netherland, J. Collins, Jessie Palmer

The G. P. Gates Company of Reserves was formed from Beat Seven. From microfilm roll number 528 on file in the Texas State Archives. This company was formed on July 11, 1861.

Officers:

G. P. Gates, Capt.; J. J. Woodard, 1st Lt.; J. F. Stephens, 2nd Lt.; W. R. Owwens, 3rd Lt.; G. D. Owens, Orderly Sgt.; J. B. Hogg, 2nd Sgt.; W. B. Hogg, 3rd Sgt.; F. Hester, 4th Sgt.; J. Reynolds, Ensign; W. D. Owens, Piper; Dorris Pierce, Drummer

Privates:

Wm. Griffin, Wm. M. Avant, S. D. K. Davis, S. V. Alexander, Robert Boyd, John Hannah, John Bowman, W. D. Pate, J. L. Owen, A. Daniel, J. Hogg, A. Hogg, John Alexander, J. M. Whitehead, R. T. Pate, J. G. Ratcliff, J. M. Palmer, John Honeycutt, A. B. Miller, G. H. Owen, Z. M. Monk, W. L. Reader, J. T. Whitehead, W. B. Crawford, R. Z. G. Cravery, John Carroll, James Carroll, James Palmer, Martin Jones, M. Sims, W. Sims, John Rice, W. J. Miller

━ ▪ ━ ▪ ━ ▪ ━ ▪ ━ ▪ ━ ▪ ━ ▪ ━ ▪ ━ ▪ ━ ▪ ━ ▪ ━ ▪ ━

Enlistment of reserves for Beat Two in Henderson County. From microfilm Number 869 in the Texas State Archives, Austin. This reserve company was formed in early March 1861.

R. B. Simpson, Hiram Neff, Yearn Tergison, Jack Colvin, A. J. McCasland, Ole Anderson, S. R. Carver, A. H. Chandler, Hassel Chandler, James Hanson, D. R. Hanison, N. Hanison, A. J. Clayton, J. S. Lindsay, Jacob Lamance, Levi Carver, John Carver, N. J. Brewer, B. Mullins, A. J. Glaze, Wm. Carver, John Cooke, J. G. Chancelor, E. Nelson, T. T. Tearfeles, Lewis Taylor, L. Shoffitt, S. D. Conary, H. C. Chambers, W. W. Majors, Aslak Tergison, Ole Gunstanson, James McParmer, Levi Boles, Turner White, Larkin Brown, (?) Cox, Gunstan Grimland, Ole Grimland, H. C. Holiman, Travis, Scott, R. Rounsavall, Nicholi Johnson, Ole Reierson, S. F. Tindle, David Brown, Joseph Echols, James Carver, Thomas Lindsay, Bud Lindsay, J. W. Cheek, James Wood, Alford Greer, Moses Greer, James McCain, Swin Olsen, Aslak Nystel, Andras Johnson, S. W. Williams, John Lindsey, Daniel Turney, Hiram Johnson, Peter Holliman, Wm. Hightower, C. Browning, J. W. Chancelor, M. Stripling, J. A. Mullen, Holly Page, D. McCain, Weston McCain, C. Norwood, J. L. Grant, (?) Knotgrass, Allen Grant, G. M. Davis, Wm. Slayton, C. P. Banks, Wm. Stamps, N. Edwards, H. F. Bridges, W. L. McNeal, A. M. Davis

━ ▪ ━ ▪ ━ ▪ ━ ▪ ━ ▪ ━ ▪ ━ ▪ ━ ▪ ━ ▪ ━ ▪ ━ ▪ ━ ▪ ━

Reserve Company for Beat One in Henderson County. List from microfilm number 869 in the Texas State Archives. Formed March 12, 1861.

W. D. Walker, Charles Ingram, P. T. Tannehill, A. S. Tannehill, S. Y. Hopper, Wm. Larkin, Wm. Brown, John R. McGill, Peter Pierce, Alfred Crosley, Berry Pierce, Wm. Knight, Wm. Kerr, Tandy Howeth, A. J. McDonald, N. Jordan, C. Jordan, Wm. C. Marquis, T. J. Hobgood, Martin Sims, John Owens, J. W. Watson, E. D. Knight, T. J. Matthews, J. E. Clark, E. Sinclair, A. S. Cox, J. M. McDonald, James Averitt, G. J. Mitcham, Elleck Mitcham, James Mitcham, Daniel Webster, S. M. Richardson, A. S. Griffith, J. T. Clark, Josiah Tidwell, John Fulton, E. Fulton, N. P. Coleman, Elijah Powell, R. S. Hines, G. W. Stephens, A. Coleman, James Smith, J. Reynolds, J. C. Larkin, J. D. Morrison, M. Richardson, C. Etheridge, Martin Jones

━ ▪ ━ ▪ ━ ▪ ━ ▪ ━ ▪ ━ ▪ ━ ▪ ━ ▪ ━ ▪ ━ ▪ ━ ▪ ━

From the muster roll for Beat Five, Henderson County, Texas 13th Brigade. Statistics from microfilm roll number 67 in the Texas State Archives. These men saw action in and around the Gulf of Mexico.

Officers:
Robert Caskey, Capt.; W. H. Wallace, 1st Lt.; T. B. Price, 2nd Lt.; J. J. Shelton, 3rd Lt.; H. A. Hodge, 2nd Sgt.; W. H. Price, 3rd Sgt.; F. F. Martin, 4th Sgt.; S. W. Shelton, 5th Sgt.; Milton Antle, 1st Cpl.; Bateman Fiske, 2nd Cpl.; F. M. Hyett, 3rd Cpl.; T. M. Tinkle, 4th Cpl.

Privates:
J. D. Anding, John Bowan, W. G. Holloway, A. J. Cox, Moses Cox, John Pickering, Wm. Pickering, S. J. Wilson, Jack Thompson, J. A. Patterson, C. D. Collins, John Robertson, R. Meddow, James Pickering, John Hannah, E. P. Walding, Robert Boyd, J. A. Goodgame, James Goodgame, John Jackson, Thomas Stuart, R. Beardon, W. W. Robertson, Martin Sims, Wm. Sims, J. Clanahan, R. D. McDaniel, Wesley Godwin, John Hambey, John Rice, S. B. Lufkin, J. Tinkle, B. Thompson, W. E. Bingham, D. Reynolds

━ ▪ ━ ▪ ━ ▪ ━ ▪ ━ ▪ ━ ▪ ━ ▪ ━ ▪ ━ ▪ ━ ▪ ━ ▪ ━

The following reserve company was mustered July 11, 1861. From microfilm number 340 located in the Texas State Archives. The men were from Beat Three, Henderson County.

Officers:
Martin W. Ross, Capt.; W. B. Stirman, 1st Lt.; B. G. Pippin, 2nd Lt.; Joab McManus, 3rd Lt.; V. I. Stirman, Orderly Sgt.; Eber Meredith, 2nd Sgt.; J. M. Pickens, 3rd Sgt.; J. M. Stirman, 4th Sgt.; Elijah Mitcham, 1st Cpl.; V. C. Choat, 2nd Cpl.; B. J. Hall, 3rd Cpl.; S. M. McManus, 4th Cpl.

Privates:

M. R. Pierson, James Weeks, M. Walker, Sylvester Walker, W. H. Mayfield, Stephen Willis, George Bell, L. B. McBride, B. F. Howard, J. A. Douglas, A. T. Perkins, W. Griffith, S. W. Green, D. N. Green, V. S. Sterman, Eli Laller, Gree Attaway, S. M. McManus, I. A. Nordain, H. L. Robertson, F. Griffith, S. Littlefield, Thomas Goodnight, J. W. Morgan, John Morgan, Henry Goodnight, Wm. Clark, James Clark, Thomas Morehead, J. Walker, W. W. Loop, W. C. Mason, A. P. Nichols, J. McNance

---

Muster roll for Beat Six Henderson County, Texas, reserve company. From microfilm roll 439 in the Texas State Archives. Mustered July 11, 1861.

Officers:

E. D. McKeller, Capt.; B. W. J. Wolford, 1st Lt.; A. T. Rice, 2nd Lt.; John C. Boles, 3rd Lt.; A. B. Oldham, 1st Sgt.; W. L. Stephenson, 2nd Sgt.; Charles C. Walker, 3rd Sgt.; Thomas Stewart, 4th Sgt.; Sam Campbell, 1st Cpl.; Jesse Winslet, 2nd Cpl.; Irwin Boles, 3rd Cpl.; B. Clifton, 4th Cpl.

Privates:

S. P. Miller, Wm. Barton, J. I. Fasen, H. H. Bishop, W. R. Wolford, N. W. Campbell, A. Rose, D. F. Pruitt, John Wassen, J. C. Oldhan, P. C. Saddler, Wm. Walker, Wm. Sullivan, N. W. Campbell, W. D. Webb, J. L. Hawley, E. W. Boles, J. D. Boles, T. J. Boles, John Faulk, S. E. Campbell, John Stewart, W. P. Stewart, Z. W. Parmer, A. J. Boles, N. T. Robertson, Wm. Smith, Axom Boles, J. J. O'Neal, J. B. Fain, S. Fain, W. G. Gauntt, J. C. Gauntt, J. M. Gauntt, T. B. Hendon, D. Champion, J. A. Knight, M. P. Blackwell, R. B. Warren, R. B. G. Fain, F. M. Casenhead, Marion Oates, F. Williams, J. C. Gore, J. H. Tare, H. Gore, James Taylor, J. M. Hopkins, John Stripling, J. A. McKeller, J. C. Oldhan, W. L. Johnson, Wm. Reynolds, W. H. Percevill, C. Percevill

---

Microfilm record number 1408 in the Texas State Archives gives the following muster roll for George Martin's Company, Reserves Militia Beat One, Henderson County, Texas. This group served in the Arkansas region during the war. Some of these men were recorded on previous list for Beat One.

Officers:

George Martin, Capt.; E. A. Carroll, 1st Lt.; J. L. Reynolds, 2nd Lt.; J. M. McDonald, 3rd Lt.; Harvey Hodge, 1st Sgt.; Wm. Davis, 2nd Sgt.; J. T. Carlisle, 3rd Sgt.; John Harper, 4th Sgt.; Jere Warren, 5th Sgt.; Isaac La Rue, 1st Cpl.; J. E. Clark, 2nd Cpl.; Wm. Helms, 3rd Cpl.

Privates:

Bernard Teah, Elbert Lley, E. Sinclair, John E. Clark, P. T. Tannehill,

Wm. Helm, J. L. Carlisle, M. E. Bonds, W. C. Marquis, L. M. Richardson, H. Morris, J. Averitt, J. Warren, J. Johns, L. Boyd, H. Hodges, W. L. Bucher, L. Y. Harper, Robert Tuggle, Jesse Foster, John Owens, A. Mitcham, J. Mitcham, John W. Dill, Wm. Price, E. G. Price, J. Wilbanks, D. L. Phase, Frank Howard, Troop Vining, S. Perry, T. B. Wood, Charles Ingram, Joel Hughes, Asa Dalton, D. McAdams, Wm. Davis, A. G. Hall, J. J. Coker, James Martin, S. Statum, A. Tannehill, C. Wilson, I. La Rue, T. Amos, N. A. Jordon, B. Pearce

▄ ▪ ▄ ▪ ▄ ▪ ▄ ▪ ▄ ▪ ▄ ▪ ▄ ▪ ▄ ▪ ▄ ▪ ▄ ▪ ▄ ▪ ▄ ▪ ▄

According to Eads, records for Company C, 34th Texas Cavalry, C. S. A. were not found in the Texas State Archives. J. J. Faulk's *History of Henderson County*, however, makes mention of them. The following is the company's muster roll as published in Faulk's book. Note many of the names are found on the rolls of other beats within the county.

Officers:

W. K. Payne, Capt.; Jim Avirett, 1st Lt.; J. W. Ballow, 2nd Lt.; W. C. Reynolds, 3rd Lt.; A. H. Chandler, 1st Sgt.; Ira Green, 2nd Sgt.; W. C. Sanders, 3rd Sgt.; Larkin Boyde, 4th Sgt.; Jim Pearce, 5th Sgt.; J. C. Chandler, 1st Cpl.; H. A. McKnight, 2nd Sgt.; Tim Burks, 3rd Cpl.; W. M. Turner, 4th Cpl.

Privates:

B. M. Ard, A. W. Davis, M. L. Alexander, H. Chandler, J. C. Andrews, John Carver, Levi Carver, W. P. Carver, W. L. Douglas, J. C. Adair, Jim Coleman, James Carlisle, John Carlisle, P. L. Bradford, W. W. Cowan, John Brown, Dick Bundy, W. Nipp, P. Johnson, Wm. Oliver, R. A. Lemons, S. M. Owens, Sam Lusk, H. C. Neal, Jim Nex, John Killen, Wm. Spikes, A. Evans, W. R. Smith, Cale Ethledge, J. P. Smith, John Fulton, John Slaughter, E. Powell, Jim Hearn, R. P. Pate, C. Ingram, Wm. Pearce, D. D. L. Jennings, W. Marcus, Jim Lendsay, T. P. Carver, W. W. Avant, W. P. Avant, W. McFarlan, J. W. Davis, Sebe Spikes, Joe Glaize, J. C. Roberts, J. M. Grant, John Reynolds, Jim Gibson, F. S. Ramby, Wm. Gerald, J. W. Reese, H. Hogg, F. Parks, W. N. Watson, A. McMullin, R. A. Davis, J. S. Davis, O. Hearn, P. Johnson, Joe Walden, J. W. McDonald, A. C. Davis, R. Malcolm, Pony Woods

Endnotes

CHAPTER 1–NOTES

1. Voter polls were established in each new county. These new polls were closer than the polls established in the old territories, thus making it possible for farmers, who could not leave their crops for any length of time, to vote.

2. Winnie McGaughey Reynolds, "The History of Henderson County" (M.A. thesis, East Texas State University, 1952), 1-2; J. J. Faulk, *History of Henderson County, Texas* (Athens, TX: Athens Review Printing Co., 1929), 31.

3. Leila Reeves Eads, ed., *Defenders: A Confederate History of Henderson County, Texas* (Athens, TX: Henderson County Historical Survey Committee, 1969), 5; Reynolds, "Henderson County," 2.

4. See Appendix One for a list of prominent citizens living in or near the city of Buffalo.

5. D & L Map Services' map of Henderson County,1995 edition, shows the different points of reference mentioned here, with the exception of Buffalo; Reynolds' "History of Henderson County," 3, indicates that Buffalo was approximately twelve miles southwest of Centerville, which in turn was located six miles west of Eustace. These figures coupled with the fact that the town would have taken advantage of the river crossing (Acker's ferry), suggest that Buffalo was located here.

6. Faulk, *Henderson County*, 10. William Ware, David Carlisle, Alfred Moore, Thatcher Vivion, Sr., and James Hooker were appointed to select a site for a seat of justice, but they never selected a place so far as the records show.

7. Faulk, *Henderson County*, 11-12; Reynolds, "Henderson County," 2. It is probable that the river was not improved upon because of the expense of such improvements. Also, toward the latter part of the 1850s, discussions regarding railroad development within the county would have overshadowed any thoughts of improving the Trinity.

8. Ibid., 3.

9. Ibid.; *A Memorial and Biographical History of Navarro, Henderson, Anderson, Limestone, Freestone, and Leon Counties, Texas* (Chicago: The Lewis Publishing Company, 1893), 201.

91

10. Jerry Chalk, "Buffalo, Henderson County, Texas, 1848-1850." Un-published paper located at the Henderson County Historical Commission, Athens, Texas: 8.

11. Faulk, *Henderson County*, 31; Reynolds, "Henderson County," 1; Eads, *Defenders*, 5.

12. Reynolds, "Henderson County," 3-4.

13. Claude Corder, ed., *1850-1860 Census of Henderson County, Texas: Including Slave Schedules and 1846 Tax List* (Chicago: Adams Press, 1984).

14. Reynolds, "Henderson County," 7.

15. Ibid., 26; Faulk, *Henderson County*, 34; Eads, *Defenders*, 1.

16. Reynolds, "Henderson County," 23; Faulk, *Henderson County*, 234.

17. Ibid., 211; Reynolds, "Henderson County," 24-25.

18. Ibid., 34; Faulk, *Henderson County*, 199.

19. Ibid., 217.

20. Ibid., 230.

21. Faulk, *Henderson County*, 281.

22. Elizabeth Silverthorne, *Plantation Life in Texas* (College Station: Texas A&M University Press, 1986) 120; Kenneth Stampp, *The Peculiar Institution: Slavery in the Ante-Bellum South* (New York: Vintage Books, 1956), 61.

23. Faulk, *Henderson County*, 281.

24. Ibid., 65.

25. Historians have divided the South into Upper and Lower regions because of the geographic, economic, social, and political differences of each area. The Upper South includes the following southern states: Maryland, Virginia, Kentucky, and, if one includes it as part of the South, Missouri. The Lower South Included: Arkansas, South Carolina, North Carolina, Georgia, Alabama, Mississippi, Louisiana, Florida, Tennessee, and Texas.

26. Walter L. Buenger, "Secession Revisited: The Texas Experience," *Civil War History* 30 (1984): 294.

27. Richard G. Lowe and Randolph B. Campbell, *Planters & Plain Folk: Agriculture in Antebellum Texas* (Dallas: Southern Methodist University Press, 1987), 13. If one only looks at the actual birthplaces of migrants, then Lowe and Campbell's conclusions are correct.

28. Seventh Census of the United States, 1850. Schedule I (Free Inhabitants) and II (Slave Inhabitants). National Archives, Washington D.C.

29. John Austin Edwards, "Social and Cultural Activities of Texans during the Civil War and Reconstruction, 1861-73," (Ph. D. dissertation: Texas Tech University, 1985), 83.

30. Ibid., 114.

31. Faulk, *Henderson County*, 68. The cemetery is probably the one located on the Thomas Parmer survey. Faulk makes reference to it in his book on page 85. He states that two and one-fourth acres of land were donated by P. T. Tannehill and N. P. Coleman in 1858 for the purpose of building a cemetery. Later, J. T. La Rue supplemented the area with the donation of an additional one-fourth of an acre. Faulk reveals to us that that the first cemetery was located on a hill in the Northeast corner of lot number 13 which was within the city limits. This is the current cemetery in use for the city of Athens. However, the

first cemetery used in Athens was located on the corner of present-day Royal Street and Old Town Alley—near the Bruce Field Stadium.

32. Ibid., 105-06.

33. Faulk, *Henderson County*, 97-99.

34. Randolph B. Campbell, *An Empire for Slavery: The Peculiar Institution in Texas, 1821-1865* (Baton Rouge: Louisiana State University Press, 1989), 171.

35. Faulk, *Henderson County*, 89-90.

36. Edwards, "Social and Cultural," 71.

37. Faulk, *Henderson County*, 97-99.

38. Ibid., 234; Reynolds, "Henderson County," 23.

39. Faulk, *Henderson County*, 72. This building was located on the east side of the present-day intersection of South Prairieville and La Rue Street.

40. Ibid., 187.

41. Ibid., 188-89.

42. Ibid.

43. Ibid.

44. Ibid.

45. C. E. Evans, *The Story of Texas Schools* (Austin: The Steck Company, 1955), 60-69. Evans' study contains a good discussion on the laws which set up the Texas public school system during the 1850s; Silverthorne, *Plantation Life*, 168.

46. Faulk, *Henderson County*, 194.

47. Ibid., 195.

48. Ibid.

49. Ibid., 195-196

50. Edwards, "Social and Cultural Activities," 12-28.

51. Faulk, *Henderson County*, 287-288.

52. Ibid., 71.

53. Ibid., 190.

54. Edwards, "Social and Cultural," 62.

55. Faulk, *Henderson County*, 302.

56. Ibid., 21-28; Minutes of the Buffalo Lyceum. Records of the County Clerk, Henderson County, Texas. (1846-1850), passim.

57. Ibid.; Faulk, *Henderson County*, 21-28.

CHAPTER 2–NOTES

1. Buenger, "Secession Revisited," 294.

2. Lowe and Campbell, *Planters & Plain Folk*, 114.

3. Seventh Census, 1850, Schedule 2; Faulk, *Henderson County*, 154-55; Eads, *Defenders*, 1.

4. Faulk, *Henderson County*, 246.

5. Seventh Census, 1850, Schedule 1. A majority of the citizens of the county held real estate valued under $500, approximately 208 acres, and owned no slaves.

6. Lowe and Campbell, *Planters & Plain Folks*, 114.

7. Seventh Census, 1850, Schedule I.

8. Faulk, *Henderson County*, 152; Berta Lowman, "Cotton Industry in Texas During the Reconstruction Period" (M. A. thesis: University of Texas at Austin, 1927), 179.

9. Faulk, *Henderson County*, 246.

10. Ibid.

11. Campbell, *Empire for Slavery*, 118.

12. Faulk, *Henderson County*, 151.

13. Lowe and Campbell, *Planters & Plain Folks*, 23.

14. Silverthorne, *Plantation Life*, 176.

15. Faulk, *Henderson County*, 246.

16. Silverthorne, *Plantation Life*, 117, estimates that it took approximately 1,500 pounds of seed cotton to make a bale. Lowe and Campbell tell their reader that most Texas counties averaged fifteen hundred pounds of seed cotton per acre. By using these two figures and Faulk's reports on cotton production, one can estimate the amount of money coming into the county and also the acreage increase.

17. Lowman, "Cotton Industry," 36.

18. Lowe and Campbell, *Planters & Plain Folks*, 18-19.

19. Ibid., 17.

20. Ibid. These bales weighed much less than the 1,500 pound field bales, because the heavy seeds, which grow naturally in cotton, were separated from the white lint fibers.

21. Silverthorne, *Plantation Life*, 117.

22. Lowe and Campbell, *Planters & Plain Folks*, 17; Faulk, *Henderson County*, 207.

23. Allen C. Ashcraft, "East Texas in the Election of 1860 and the Secession Crisis," *East Texas Historical Journal* 1 (July 1963): 7.

24. Faulk, *Henderson County*, 283.

25. Lowe and Campbell, *Planters and Plain Folks*, 189.

26. Faulk, *Henderson County*, 65-280 passim.

27. Ibid.; Silverthorne, *Plantation Life*, 105.

28. Faulk, *Henderson County*, 246.

29. Ibid., 66.

30. Ralph A. and Robert Wooster, "A People at War: East Texans during the Civil War," East Texas Historical Journal 28 (1990): 8-9; Katheryn Brown, unfinished manuscript on the history of Henderson County. Located at the Henderson County Historical Commission Office in the Henderson County Court House, Athens, Texas.

31. Faulk, *Henderson County*, 247.

32. Ibid., 75.

33. Ibid., 66.

34. Ibid., 74; Ralph A. Wooster, "Life in Civil War East Texas," *East Texas Historical Journal* 3 (October 1965): 97.

35. Faulk, *Henderson County*, 69.

36. The *Texas Almanac for 1857* (Galveston: Richardson & Co., 1856), 69; Eads, *Defenders*, 6; Campbell, *Empire for Slavery*, 265; Seventh Census, 1850, Schedule 1 and 2; Eighth Census, 1860, Schedule 1 and 2.

37. Ibid.; Seventh Census, 1850, Schedule 1 and 2.

38. Rupert Richardson, Ernest Wallace, and Adrian Anderson, Texas: The *Lone Star State* (Englewood Cliffs: Prentice Hall, 1943), 245.

39. John W. Blassingame, *The Slave Community: Plantation Life in the Antebellum South* (New York: Oxford University Press, 1972), 251. Slaves belonging to a yeoman farmer remained under close supervision in much the same way that slaves working as domestic servants remained under the watchful eye of the larger planters.

40. Eighth Census, 1860, Schedule 1 and 2.

41. Reynolds, "Henderson County," 120, discusses wealth and migration of slaves briefly. On page 18 the author mentions the agricultural abundance of Fincastle.

42. Blassingame, *The Slave Community*, 249-283 passim.

43. Campbell, *1* 224.

44. Reynolds, "Henderson County," 120-21; William W. White, "The Texas Slave Insurrection in 1860," *The Southwestern Historical Quarterly* 52 (January 1949): 272.

45. Part of Dr. Donald E. Reynold's lecture on the Old South, History 561, East Texas State University, Spring 1995. These newly developed matches ignited after long term exposure to the extreme temperatures of the Texas summer. It was reported that temperatures in Texas during the summer of 1859 climbed higher than 110 degrees.

46. Reynolds, "Henderson County," 120-121; For newspaper accounts of the incident with Wyrick and Cable see the *Tyler Reporter*, August 8, 1860 quoted by the *Austin State Gazette*, August 25, 1860 or the *Fairfield Pioneer*, August 9, 1860 quoted by the *New Orleans Daily Picayune*, August 14, 1860.

CHAPTER 3–NOTES

1. Ralph A. Wooster, "East of the Trinity River: Glimpses of life in East Texas in the Early 1850's," *East Texas Historical Journal* 13 (Fall 1975): 7; Randolph B. Campbell, *A Southern Community in Crisis: Harrison County, Texas, 1850-1880* (Austin: Texas State Historical Association, 1983), 178. Both authors agree that the wealthy people of East Texas were the political leaders within their respective communities.

2. O. M. Roberts, "The Political, Legislative, and Judicial History of Texas for Its Fifty Years of Statehood, 1845-1895," in *A Comprehensive History of Texas 1845 to 1897*, ed. Dudley G. Wooten (Dallas: William G. Scarff, 1898), 21. See Appendix Two for a list of Henderson County's local politicians.

3. Ben Procter, *Not Without Honor: The Life of John H. Reagan* (Austin: University of Texas Press, 1962), 61-62.

4. Waymon L. McClellan, "1855: The Know-Nothing Challenge in East Texas," *East Texas Historical Journal* 12 (Fall 1974): 26. Between 1850 and 1860 the white population increased by 201 percent, but during the same time the slave population increased 1,277 percent.

5. Campbell, *Community in Crisis*, 157. Campbell's study is based on Harrison County, however, his analysis of the political atmosphere in that county has wider application in East Texas as a whole.

6. Ibid., 178-179.

7. Ibid., 176; Mike Kingston, Sam Attlesey, and Mary G. Crawford, *The Texas Almanac's Political History of Texas* (Austin: Eakin Press, 1992), 51, 55, 73. Twenty-three out of ninety-seven voters cast ballots for Winfield Scott, a Whig candidate, in the presidential election of 1852. Seventy-five votes out of 367 were given to the Whig's candidate, Millard Fillmore, in the presidential election of 1856. In 1860, 120 of 584 votes cast went to John Bell of the Constitutional Union Party. Voting at the state levels followed the national trends with a minority of the votes going to candidates associated with opposition parties.

8. *Trinity Advocate* (Palestine), 12 May 1858.

9. Campbell, *Community in Crisis*, 148; Kingston, *Political History*, 73; Henderson County election records at the Texas State Library and Archives Commission. In the 1852 presidential election ninety-seven people from Henderson County voted. A year before in the state congressional election 140 voters cast ballots. However, in pivotal national elections, such as the 1860 presidential election, Henderson County's voter participation was closely aligned to that of elections held the year prior at the state level.

10. Ibid., 153.

11. Based on the numerous court settlements published in the *Trinity Advocate*, there can be little doubt that prosperous landowners wanted to maintain personal influence with the courtroom judges.

12. Campbell, *Community in Crisis*, 149.

13. Ibid. Campbell's descriptions of Harrison County political offices could describe any county within Texas during this time.

14. Reynolds, "Henderson County," 2.

15. *A Memorial and Biographical History*, 201.

16. Reynolds, "Henderson County," 5.

17. Seventh Census, 1850, Schedule 1. The figures used to describe the economic, social, and physical conditions of the members of the 1850 Commissioners' Court were all found in the census records. These figures were compiled from a study of seven members of the 1850 Commissioners' Court—Chief Justice M. C. Howard who filled that office until the election of E. M. Curtis, County Clerk E. J. Thompson, Sheriff W. H. Gray, Commissioners J. B. Luker, Durham Avant, and Thomas Helm.

18. Seventh Census, 1850, Schedule 1; Eighth Census, 1860, Schedule 1.

19. Ibid. The figures used to describe the conditions of the 1857 court members were taken from the census records. The figures were compiled from a study of six members in the 1857 Commissioners' Court. They are as follows: Chief Justice J. B. Luker, County Clerk E. J. Thompson, Commissioners S. Richardson, K. K. Knight, W. R. Clark, and Thomas Berry.

20. Eighth Census, 1860, Schedule 1. The information used for these figures was based on a study of eight individuals—Chief Justice D. A. Owens, County Clerk Perry Warren, J. E. Thompson, J. M. Stirman, John D. Morrison, Sheriff E. A. Carroll, and Commissioners W. W. Carver, J. A. Goodgame, W. K. Faulk, and Nat P. Coleman.

21. Llerena Friend, *Sam Houston: The Great Designer* (Austin: University of Texas Press, 1954), 193; Roberts, "History of Texas," 27. Both authors clearly define the issues in Texas politics during the 1850s.

22. T. R. Fehrenbach, *Lone Star: A History of Texas and the Texans* (New York: Wing Books, 1968), 280.

23. Dorman H. Winfrey and James M. Day, ed., *The Indian Papers of Texas and the Southwest* (Austin: The Pemberton Press, 1966), vol. 3, 102-103. This report was evident from a letter sent to the citizens of Navarro County from Governor Wood, assuring them he would do everything possible to keep the Indians from crossing the frontier line.

24. Rupert Richardson, Ernest Wallace, and Adrian Anderson, *Texas: The Lone Star State* (Englewood Cliffs: Prentice Hall, 1943), 170. The authors estimate this to be the location of Texas' frontier line during this time.

25. Fehrenbach, *Lone Star*, 277. Fehrenbach reveals the dilemma Texas faced. It had vast amounts of land but was having to give it away in order to encourage settlement in certain parts of the state, especially along the frontier.

26. Roberts, "History of Texas," 27.

27. John H. Reagan, *Memoirs with Special References to Secession and the Civil War*, ed. by Walter Flavius McCaleb (New York: The Neale Publishing Company, 1906), 52.

28. Roberts, "History of Texas," 29.

29. Friend, *Sam Houston*, 194-95.

30. Emilia Gay Means, "East Texas and the Trans–Continental Railroad," *East Texas Historical Journal* 25 (1987): 49-51.

31. Lewis W. Newton and Herbert P. Gambrell, *A Social and Political History of Texas* (Dallas: Southwest Press, 1932), 246.

32. Kingston, *Political History*, 51.

33. Robert G. Winchester, *James Pickney Henderson: Texas First Governor* (San Antonio: The Naylor Company, 1971), 94.

34. The more strident form of southern politics was a political ideology formed by Southerners who wanted to protect the rights of slaveowners and maintain the South's dominant position in the United States Government throughout the 1850s.

35. Kingston, *Political History*, 51 and 55. The county's limited support for gubernatorial candidates like B. H. Epperson in 1851 and W. B. Ochiltree in 1853 suggests only a small number of the county's voters were Whigs.

36. Ibid.

37. Roberts, "History of Texas," 37. Roberts reveals how D. C. Dickson could have been endorsed by the Know-Nothings but still ran as a Democratic candidate. Two weeks before Dickson's endorsement by the Know-Nothings, he was nominated to run on the Democratic ticket for lieutenant governor; *New Handbook of Texas*, Vol. 2, 638. Strengthens the argument that Dickson, who was merely endorsed by the American party (Know-Nothing party), remained a staunch Democrat; William D. Overdyke, *The Know-Nothing Party in the South* (Baton Rouge: Louisiana State University Press, 1950), 116-117. Overdyke reveals that Dickson endorsed state owned railways and the Texas Debt Bill which provided a way to pay outstanding state debts by selling state owned lands. These particular views would have appealed to the Whig Party.

38. *Trinity Advocate* (August 21, 1859) shows the election results for the county. Houston received 300 votes to the Democratic candidate Hardin Runnels' 191.

39. Philip J. Avillo, Jr., "John H. Reagan: Unionist or Secessionist?" *East Texas Historical Journal* 13 (Spring 1975): 24.

40. Kingston, *Political History*, 73.

41. Patsy McDonald Spaw, The Texas Senate: Volume I, *Republic to Civil War, 1836-1861* (College Station: Texas A&M University Press, 1990), 301. Spaw writes that state's rights leaders had won the upper hand on almost every political front in Texas in 1859; Seymour V. Connor and Willaim Pool, *Texas: The 28th Star* (Austin: Graphic Ideas, Inc., 1972), 83. Connor also states Breckinridge's victory in Texas illustrates a definite shift toward secession. A shift proving that Texas party machinery was controlled by secessionists.

CHAPTER 4–NOTES

1. Almost every Houston biography points out that Houston had political aspirations for the presidency. Many Southerners during the 1850s argued that only possible way to successfully achieve his goal was to maintain popularity with northern states and at the same time champion the rights of his own section, the South. Such views, of course, overlook the fact that Houston was a man of principles, who strongly favored preserving the Union.

2. Part of Dr. Donald E. Reynold's lectures on the Old South, History 561, East Texas State University, Spring 1995.

3. See Chapter Two, pages 45-46 for more details.

4. Campbell, *Empire for Slavery*, 184-185.

5. Avillo, "John Reagan," 24.

6. Buenger, "Secession Revisited," 296.

7. Ibid.

8. Ibid. Buenger describes each of the four attitudes toward the Union in greater detail in this article.

9. *Trinity Advocate* (August 21, 1859). Voter returns for this election can be found in this edition. Houston collected 300 votes to Runnels' 191.

10. Robert F. Diamond, ed., *National Party Conventions, 1831-1972* (Washington, D.C.: Congressional Quarterly Inc., 1976), 32.

11. Roberts, "History of Texas," 78.

12. Campbell, *Community in Crisis*, 196.

13. Buenger, "Secession Revisited," 298.

14. Campbell, *Community in Crisis*, 197. Campbell contends that response to radical abolitionist rhetoric and a distrust of the northern industrial society caused Southerners to blur the distinctions between the two groups. Republicans wanted to stop the expansion of slavery; thus, their presidential candidate, Lincoln, was labeled an abolitionist.

15. Buenger, "Secession Revisted," 298.

16. Ibid., 297-299.

17. Ibid., 295.

18. Campbell, *Community in Crisis*, 192-193.

19. Roberts, "History of Texas," 73.

20. Ibid., 83.

21. Faulk, *Henderson County*, 56.

22. James Allen Marten, *Texas Divided: Loyalty and Dissent in the Lone Star State, 1856-1874* (Lexington: University Press of Kentucky, 1990), 21.

23. Buenger, "Secession Revisted," 299-301.

24. Roberts, "History of Texas," 79.

25. Ibid., 83.

26. *Members of the Texas State Legislature*, 32-35; *New Handbook of Texas*, Vol. 4, 1049.

27. Ibid., 527; *Members of the Texas State Legislature*, 23-25; Spaw, *The Texas Senate*, 301-322 and 361.

28. Randolph B. Campbell, *Sam Houston and the American Southwest* (New York: Harper Collins College Publishers, 1993), 151.

29. Roberts, "History of Texas," 86-98. Roberts gives a detailed account of the Secession Convention and the events which preceded and followed it.

30. Marten, *Texas Divided*, 20-21. Marten reveals the vote for secession was 166 for to 8 against. This is not surprising considering that unionists found an uneasy welcome at this convention.

31. Joe T. Timmons, "Texas on the Road to Secession" (Ph.D. Dissertation: University of Chicago, 1973), 784-785.

32. Buenger, "Secession Revisited," 299.

33. Ibid., 305.

34. Eads, *Defenders*, 1. Eads reveals that the secession vote in Henderson County was 397 for and 48 against. It must be noted that Eads' figures are slightly inaccurate when compared to the election returns of February 23, 1861. The actual count was was 400 for and 49 opposed; *A Memorial and Biographical History*, 205. This source gives a sketchy account of the secession movement in Henderson County.

35. Jack Stoltz, "Kaufman County in the Civil War" East Texas Historical Journal 28 (1990): 37. Stoltz states that Kaufman voted in favor of secession 461 to 155; Wooster, "A People at War," 4. Wooster found that 90 percent of the voters in the counties of Smith and Anderson were for secession, while 40 percent of the voters in Van Zandt voted against it.

36. Ashcraft, "Secession Crisis," 13.

CHAPTER 5–NOTES

1. United States Census, 1850 and 1860, Schedule I and Schedule II. In 1850 there were 256 men who were twenty years old or older living within the county. Of these 256, twenty-three were slaveholders (9 percent of the population). In 1860 there were 258 men who were twenty years old or older. Of these 258, 161 were slaveholders (62 percent of the population).

2. Ina Woestemeyer Van Noppen, ed. *The South: A Documentary History* (Princeton: D. Van Nostrand Company, Inc., 1958), 168; Laurence Shore, *Southern Capitalists: The Ideological Leadership of an Elite, 1832-1885* (Chapel Hill: The University of North Carolina Press, 1986), 46. Both historians mention the displacement of the yeoman farmers along the frontier.

3. Charles S. Sydnor, *The Development of Southern Sectionalism, 1819-1848*, A History of the South Series, ed. Wendell Holmes Stephenson and E. Merton Coulter, no. 5 (Baton Rouge: Louisiana State University Press), 294.

4. Ibid., 304.

5. R. S. Cotterill, *The Old South: The Geographic, Economic, Political, and Cultural Expansion, Institutions, and Nationalism of the Ante-bellum South* (Glendale: The Arthur H. Clark Company, 1939), 293-314. Cotterill's study gives a good overall picture of the South's literary world.

6. See Chapter Two of this study for more information regarding the county's production of cotton; John Solomon Otto, *The Southern Frontiers, 1607-1860: The Agricultural Evolution of the Colonial and Antebellum South* (New York: Greenwood Press, 1989), 104. Henderson County fits into the same categories as other southern frontier upland regions described by Otto. These areas included: piedmont Georgia, central and northern Alabama, central and northeastern Mississippi, eastern, middle and western Tennessee, central and western Kentucky, and central and eastern Missouri.

7. Ibid., 129-130.

8. Shore, *Capitalists*, 48.

9. David Brion Davis, *The Fear of Conspiracy: Images of Un-American Subversion from the Revolution to the Present* (Ithaca: Cornell University Press, 1971), 106, and *The Slave Power Conspiracy and the Paranoid Style* (Baton Rouge: Louisiana State University Press, 1969), 35; Eugene D. Genovese, *Roll, Jordan, Roll: The World The Slaves Made* (New York: Pantheon Books, 1972), 588-589. Genovese states that the revolts of the Old South did compare in size, frequency, intensity, or historical significance with those of the Caribbean.

10. Davis, *The Fear of Conspiracy*, 106; Davis, *The Slave Power Conspiracy*, 35.

11. Genovese, *Roll, Jordan, Roll*, 588.

12. Davis, *Slave Power Conspiracy*, 39.

13. For more information regarding this incident see Chapter Two of this study.

14. Davis, *Slave Power Conspiracy*, 57.

15. For more details concerning Henderson County's politics see Chapters Three and Four of this study.

16. Frank Smyrl, "Unionism in Texas, 1856-1861," *The Southwestern Historical Quarterly* 48 (1965): 172-195. Smyrl gives an overall account of Unionism in Texas during the latter part of the 1850s.

17. See Appendix Three for a complete list of volunteer militia and reserve groups from Henderson County.

CHAPTER 6–NOTES

1. A copy of the "Old Settlers Edition" can be found at the Henderson County Historical Commission, Athens, Texas.

2. The biographical sketch of William H. Martin comes from a paper presented by Professor Claude Hall of Texas A&M University at the fifth annual meeting of the East Texas Historical Association, October 7, 1967, at Nacogdoches, Texas.

Bibliography

Primary Sources

Memories, Reminiscences, Journals, Diaries, and Historical Accounts by Participants

De Cordova, J. *Texas: Her Resources and Her Public Men*. Philadelphia: J. B. Lippincott & Co., 1958.

Fremantle, James Arthur Lyon. *The Fremantle Diary: Being the Journal of Lieutenant Colonel James A. L. Fremantle, Coldstream Gaurds, on His Three Months in the Southern States*. Edited by Walter Lord. Boston: Little, Brown, and Co., 1954.

Lubbock, Francis R. *Six Decades in Texas: The Memoirs of Francis R. Lubbock, Confederate Governer of Texas*. Edited by C. W. Raines. Austin: The Pemberton Press, 1968.

Olmsted, Frederick Law. *A Journey Through Texas: or, a Saddle-trip on the Southwestern Frontier*. New York, 1857; reprint, Austin: University of Texas Press, 1978.

Rawick, George P., ed. *The American Slave: A Composite Autobiography*. Vols. 4 and 5. Westport: Greenwood Publishing Company, 1941.

Reagan, John H. *Memoirs with Special References to Secession and the Civil War*. Edited by Walter Flavius McCaleb. New York: The Neale Publishing Company, 1906.

Roberts, O. M. "The Political, Legislative, and Judicial History of Texas for Its Fifty Years of Statehood, 1845-1895." In *A Comprehensive History of Texas, 1845-1897*. Edited by Dudley G. Wooten, 7-325. Dallas: William G. Scarff, 1898.

Government Documents

Inventories and Appraisements. Records of the County Clerk, Athens, Henderson County, Texas. Book B2.

Minutes of the Buffalo Lyceum. Records of the County Clerk, Henderson County, Texas (1846-1850).

United States Bureau of the Census. *Eighth Census of the United States, 1860: Schedule I and II.* National Archives, Washington, D.C.

————. *Seventh Census of the United States, 1850: Schedule I and II.* National Archives, Washington, D.C.

Winfrey, Dorman H. and James M. Day, eds. *The Indians Papers of Texas and the Southwest.* Vol. 3. Austin: The Pemberton Press, 1966.

News Papers

Trinity Advocate (Palestine, TX), 1857-1860.

"Old Settlers Edition" *Athens Review* (Athens, TX), August 2, 1901.

Almanacs

The Texas Almanacs for 1857 with Statistics. Galveston: Richardson & Co., 1856; reprint, Dallas: A. H. Belo Corporation, 1966.

Secondary Sources

Unpublished Manuscripts, Papers and Lectures

Chalk, Jerry. "Buffalo, Henderson County, Texas, 1846-1850." Unpublished manuscript, Henderson County Historical Commission, Athens, Texas.

Collier, G. Loyd. "The Evolving East Texas Woodlands." Ph.D. diss., University of Nebraska, 1964.

Brown, Katheryn. Unfinished manuscipt on the history of Henderson County. Henderson County Historical Commission, Athens, Texas.

Edwards, John Austin. "Social and Cultural Activities of Texans during the Civil War and Reconstruction, 1861-73." Ph.D. diss., Texas Tech University, 1985.

Elam, Richard Lee. "Behold the Fields: Texas Baptists and the Problem of Slavery." Ph.D. diss., University of North Texas, 1993.

Hall, Claude. "Congressman William H. 'Howdy' Martin." A paper read at the Fifth Annual meeting of the East Texas Historical Association, October 7, 1967, at Nacogdoches, Texas.

Lowman, Berta. "Cotton Industry in Texas during the Reconstruction Period." M.A. thesis, University of Texas at Austin, 1927.

Reynolds, Donald E. Lectures on the Old South, History 561, East Texas State University, Spring 1995.

Reynolds, Winnie McGaughey. "The History of Henderson County." M.A. thesis, East Texas University, 1952.

Robinson, Florence. "History of Education in Henderson County, Texas." M.A. thesis, Southern Methodist University, 1940.

Smallwood, James M. Unpublished manuscript on the history of Smith County. Copy in the author's possession.

Timmons, Joe T. "Texas on the Road to Secession." Ph.D. diss., University of Chicago, 1973.

Books

Blassingame, John W. *The Slave Community: Plantation Life in the Antebellum South*. New York: Oxford University Press, 1972.

Buenger, Walter L. *Secession and the Union in Texas*. Austin: University of Texas Press, 1984.

Campbell, Randolph B. *An Empire for Slavery: The Peculiar Institution in Texas, 1821-1865*. Baton Rouge: Louisiana State University Press, 1989.

———. *Sam Houston and the American Southwest*. New York: Harper Collins College Publishers, 1993.

———. *A Southern Community in Crisis: Harrison County, Texas, 1850-1880*. Austin: Texas State Historical Association, 1983.

Connor, Seymour V. *Texas: A History*. New York: Thomas Y. Crowell Company, 1971.

——— and William C. Pool. *Texas: The 28th Star*. Austin: Graphic Ideas, Inc., 1972.

Corder, Estelle, ed. *1850-1860 Census of Henderson County, Texas: Including Slave Schedules and 1846 Tax List*. Chicago: Adams Press, 1984.

Cotterill, R. S. *The Old South: The Geographic, Economic, Political, and Cultural Expansion, Institutions, and Nationalism of the Ante-bellum South*. Glendale: The Arthur H. Clark Company, 1939.

Davis, David Brion, ed. *The Fear of Conspiracy: Images of Un-American Subversion from the Revolution to the Present*. Ithaca: Cornell University Press, 1969.

———. *The Slave Power Conspiracy and the Paraanoid Style*. Baton Rouge: Louisiana State University Press, 1969.

Diamond, Robert, A., ed. *National Party Conventions, 1831-1972*. Washington, D.C.: Congressional Quarterly Inc., 1976.

Divine, Robert, T. H. Breen, George M. Fredrickson, R. Hal Williams, and Randy Roberts. *America: Past and Present*. Third brief edition. New York: Harper Collins College Publishers, 1994.

Durden, Robert F. *The Self-Inflicted Wound: Southern Politics in the Nineteenth Century*. Lexington: The University Press of Kentucky, 1985.

Eads, Leila Reeves, ed. *Defenders: A Confederate History of Henderson County, Texas*. Athens, TX: Henderson County Historical Survey Committee, 1969.

Evans, Cecil E. *The Story of Texas Schools*. Austin: The Steck Company, 1955.

Family Histories of Henderson County Texas 1846-1981: A Collection of Family Sketches and Biographies of the People of Henderson County. Dallas: Taylor Publishing Co., 1981.

Faulk, J. J. *History of Henderson County Texas*. Athens, TX: Athens Review Printing Co., 1929.

Fehrenbach, T. R *Lone Star: A History of Texas and the Texans*. New York: Wing Books, 1968.

Friend, Llerena. *Sam Houston: The Great Designer*. Austin: University of Texas Press, 1954.

Genovese, Eugene D. *Roll, Jordan, Roll: The World Slaves Made*. New York: Pantheon Books, 1972.

Hall, Margaret Elizabeth. *A History of Van Zandt County*. Austin: Jenkins Publishing Company, 1976.

Kingston, Mike, Sam Attlesey, and Mary G. Crawford. *The Texas Almanac's Political History of Texas*. Austin: Eakin Press, 1992.

Kittrell, Norman G. *Governors Who Have Been, and Other Public Men of Texas*. Houston: Dealy-Adey-Elgin, Co., 1921.

Lowe, Richard G. and Randolph B. Campbell. *Planters & Plain Folk: Agriculture in Antebellum Texas*. Dallas: Southern Methodist University Press, 1987.

Marten, James A. *Texas Divided: Loyalty and Dissent in the Lone Star State, 1856-1874*. Lexington: University Press of Kentucky, 1990.

A Memorial and Biographical History of Navarro, Henderson, Anderson, Limestone, Freestone, and Leon Counties, Texas. Chicago: The Lewis Publishing Company, 1893.

Newton, Lewis W. and Herbert P. Gambrell. *A Social and Political History of Texas*. Dallas: Southwest Press, 1931.

Otto, John Solomon. *The Southern Frontiers, 1607-1806: The Agricultural Evolution of the Colonial and Antebellum South*. New York: Greenwood Press, 1989.

Overdyke, William D. *The Know-Nothing Party in the South*. Baton Rouge: Louisiana State University Press, 1950.

Patman, Wright. *A History of Post Offices and Communities: First Congressional District of Texas*. Texarkana, TX: Privately printed, 1990.

Phares, Ross. *The Governors of Texas*. Gretna: Pelican Publishing Company, 1976.

Procter, Ben. *Not Without Honor: The Life of John H. Reagan*. Austin: University of Texas Press, 1962.

Richardson, Rupert, Ernest Wallace, and Adrian Anderson. *Texas: The Lone Star State*. Englewood Cliffs: Prentice Hall, 1943.

Richardson, T. C. *East Texas: Its History and Its Makers*. Edited by Dobney White. Vol 1. New York: Lewis Historical Publishing Company, 1940.

Shore, Laurence. *Southern Capitalists: The Ideological Leadership of an Elite, 1832-1885*. Chapel Hill: The University of North Carolina Press, 1986.

Silverthorne, Elizabeth. *Plantation Life in Texas*. College Station: Texas A&M University Press, 1986.

Spaw, Patsy McDonald, ed. *The Texas Senate: Volume I, Republic to Civil War, 1836-1861*. College Station: Texas A&M University Press, 1990.

Stampp, Kenneth. *The Peculiar Institution: Slavery in the Ante-Bellum South.* New York: Vintage Books, 1956.

Syndor, Charles S. *The Development of Southern Sectionalism 1819-1848.* A History of the South Series, ed. Wendell Holmes Stephenson and E. Merton Coulter, No. 5. Baton Rouge: Louisiana State University Press, 1948.

Texas State Legislature. *Members of the Texas Legislature, 1846-1962.* Austin: Legislature, 1962.

Tyler, Ron, Douglas E. Barnett, Roy R. Barkley, Penelope C. Anderson, and Mark F. Odintz, eds. *The New Handbook of Texas.* Austin: The Texas State Historical Association, 1996.

United States Bureau of Census. *Historical Statistics of the United States, Colonial Times to 1970, Bicentennial Edition.* 2 Vols. Washington, D.C.: Government Printing Office, 1975.

United States Census Office. *Statistics of the United States in 1860 Complied from the Original Returns of the Eighth Census.* New York: Aron Press, 1976.

Van Noppen, Ina Woestemeyer, ed. *The South: A Documentary History.* Princeton: D. Van Nostrand Company, Inc., 1958.

Volz, Vandace, ed. *Texana II: Cultural Heritage of the Plantation South.* Austin: Texas Historical Commission, 1982.

Webb, Walter Prescott, ed. *The Handbook of Texas.* 2 vols. Austin: The Texas State Historical Association, 1952.

Winchestor, Robert Glenn. *James Pinckney Henderson: Texas First Governor.* San Antonio: The Naylor Company, 1971.

Wooster, Ralph A. *The Secession Conventions of the South.* Princeton: Princeton University Press, 1962.

Articles

Ashcraft, Allan C. "East Texas in the Election of 1860 and the Secession Crisis." *East Texas Historical Journal* 1 (July 1963): 7-15.

Avillo, Phlip J., Jr. "John H. Reagan: Unionist or Secessionist?" *East Texas Historical Journal* 13 (Spring 1975): 23-33.

Buenger, Walter L. "Secession Revisted: The Texas Experience." *Civil War History* 30 (1984):293-305.

McClellan, Waymon L. "1855: The Know-Nothing Challenge in East Texas." *East Texas Historical Journal* 12 (Fall 1974): 32-44.

Means, Emilia Gay. "East Texas and the Transcontinental Railroad." *East Texas Historical Journal* 25 (1987): 49-59.

Smyrl, Frank H. "Unionism in Texas, 1856-1861." *The Southwestern Historical Quarterly* 48 (1965): 172-195.

Stolz, Jack. "Kaufman County in the Civil War." *East Texas Historical Journal* 28 (1990): 37- 44.

White, William. "The Texas Slave Insurrection in 1860." *The Southwestern Historical Quarterly* 52 (January 1949): 259-285.

Wooster, Ralph A. "East of the Trinity: Glimpses of Life in East Texas in the Early 1850s." *East Texas Historical Journal* 13 (Fall 1975): 3-10.

———. "Life in Civil War East Texas." *East Texas Historical Journal* (October 1965): 93-102

——— and Robert Wooster. "A People at War: East Texans during the Civil War." *East Texas Historical Journal* 28 (1990): 3-16.

Maps

Map of Henderson County. Arlington, Texas: D & L Map Service, 1995.

Photocopy of a map of Henderson County (1850s). Part of Katheryn Brown's unpublished manuscript. Henderson County Historical Commission, Athens, Texas.

Index

www.ingramcontent.com/pod-product-compliance
Lightning Source LLC
Chambersburg PA
CBHW030844090426

42737CB00009B/1101